CONFIDENCE
to Care

A Resource for Family Carers Providing
Alzheimer's Disease or Other Dementias Care at Home

MOLLY CARPENTER

Home Instead Press

D0265620

Disclaimer:

Please note that the content, suggestions and tips included in this resource are provided for informational purposes only. They are not intended to be and should not be construed as being medical advice or a substitute for receiving professional medical advice, diagnosis or treatment. Always seek the advice of a physician or other qualified medical provider for any questions you or a loved one may have regarding a medical condition.

Home Instead Press, LLC, Home Instead, Inc. and the Home Instead Senior Care® franchise and master franchise network do not warrant or guarantee that following any of the suggestions or tips included in this resource will help to prevent, eliminate or alleviate any of the behavioural or other symptoms associated with persons who suffer from dementia, and expressly disclaim any liability with respect to the content, suggestions and tips included in this resource.

Contents

· · · · · · · · · · · · · · · · · · ·

Acknowledgments

We gratefully acknowledge the efforts of these individuals without whom this book could not have been possible. Our expert content panel:

Bob Bird M.A., a Home Instead Senior Care® franchise owner from Wilmington, Delaware, who has worked extensively in the field of dementia care; C. Angela Burrow CDP, AP-BC, RN, SCM, a Certified National Trainer at the Learning Community for Person Centered Practices at the University of North Carolina-Chapel Hill and a Nationally Certified Dementia Practitioner; and Kathy Laurenhue M.A., CEO of Wiser Now, Inc., a writer, trainer and curriculum developer.

In addition, our sincere appreciation goes out to our review panel:

Dr. Jane Potter, Professor and Chief of Geriatrics and Gerontology in the Department of Medicine, University of Nebraska Medical Centre; David Troxel MPH, internationally known writer and teacher in the fields of Alzheimer's disease and long-term care; Tanya Richmond, Program Coordinator and an Assistant Clinical Professor with the Centre for Ageing Research and Educational Services; Dr. Amy D'Aprix, M.S.W., Ph.D., CSA, a Life Transition Consultant, author, professional speaker and expert in ageing, retirement and caregiving.

Thanks to our creative team who helped consult, coordinate, research, write and design this book, including Jim Beck, Georgene Lahm, Rachel Lambert, Kami Manstedt, Alex McCann and Jenny Witt.

Our thanks also go to The Dilenschneider Group and Significance Press, with special appreciation to Joe Tessitore, Joe Pisani and Patrick Malone for their encouragement and publishing expertise. Thanks also to our editor, Jim Zebora.

We also extend our appreciation to the following Home Instead, Inc., individuals and business partners who contributed their advice, assistance and especially encouragement, including Jessie Brumbach, Erin Albers, Greg Skolaut, Dan Wieberg, Albers Communications Group, Fleishman-Hillard U.S. and Canada, and Immersion Active.

In addition, we appreciate the many individuals who shared personal stories about their experience with Alzheimer's disease or other dementias along with care tips from family carers, as well as staff and CAREGivers[SM] throughout the Home Instead Senior Care network.

Finally, our sincere appreciation to Home Instead, Inc., franchisor of the Home Instead Senior Care network, for its vision and thought leadership in bringing this valuable resource to family carers.

Foreword

As we write this, we can't help but think about the estimated 35 million families around the world facing the realities of caring for someone with Alzheimer's disease. For each, it must seem like the greatest challenge of their lives.

You may be one of them – wondering how to help your gentle father who is suddenly showing fits of anger, or your mother who wanders at night, putting herself at risk and keeping you awake with worry.

For most family carers, caring for someone with Alzheimer's disease or other dementias is a new and intimidating experience.

Without knowing what triggers behaviours or some practical techniques to counter them, it's easy to feel overwhelmed.

It has been nearly 20 years now, but our first experience with Alzheimer's disease is still crystal clear in our memories. We had just opened the first Home Instead Senior Care® office to provide in-home care for older people. One of our CAREGivers – very frustrated – called to ask for advice. "How can I get Marion to change clothes?" she wanted to know. "She insists on wearing the same grey trouser suit every day, all day."

How we wish that we knew then what we know now! What a difference it would have made in helping our CAREGiver find a way to get Marion into a fresh set of clothes. We would have simply told her daughter to buy a duplicate of her mother's favourite grey trouser suit.

And that, of course, is why we are publishing this book – to give you practical advice so that you can confidently face caring for someone with Alzheimer's disease at home. It's based on two decades of experience working with and supporting people with Alzheimer's disease or other dementias. We've also asked some of the most respected experts in dementia care to share their insights so people like you can be successful in providing care for Alzheimer's disease or other dementias at home. Some of the best advice in this book came, not surprisingly, from family carers who shared generously from their own experiences to help you.

At this moment, there are two sobering facts about Alzheimer's disease. First, our world is experiencing an Alzheimer's epidemic. Second, in spite of an enormous investment of time, money and medical talent, no cure or prevention for Alzheimer's disease has been found and none is expected in the foreseeable future.

But, while there is no cure, there is care!

For almost every family, that care begins at home and is provided by someone just like you. Without training, most are likely unfamiliar with dementia in any form, and already over-committed with children and a job. Still, they are totally committed to caring for Mum or Dad out of love and a sense of responsibility.

If that's you, then you are exactly the person for whom we've written this book.

Through our work in providing care to tens of thousands of people with dementia, we've learnt that the behavioural symptoms sometimes exhibited by those with the disease are also the most frustrating to deal with. So with this book we want to help you understand what may cause those behaviours, how to deal with them, and what you can do to help prevent or alleviate them.

We also understand that there can be emotional and physical consequences for carers who often find themselves providing care day after day, month after month and sometimes, year after year. So, we have included advice about how to care for yourself. Read this chapter first, because you can't care for Mum unless you are taking care of yourself.

If you need or would like additional advice, we encourage you to make use of the resources listed in the back of this book. Also, the Home Instead Senior Care network offers special training for family carers. It's the same Alzheimer's Disease or Other Dementias CARE: Changing Ageing Through Research and Education® training that the network provides to its professional CAREGivers. It's free, and you can take advantage of it in two ways. First, just watch the short training videos on our website (see Alzheimer's & Dementia Care tab). Or you can join one of our family workshops when it is offered in your area by contacting your local Home Instead Senior Care office.

In the end, we trust that by reading this book you will become a more confident carer. Confidence leads to better care and makes the privilege of caring more fulfilling. It is our deepest desire that "Confidence to Care" will help you experience these outcomes.

Finally, thank you for caring. As a family carer, you have taken on one of the most rewarding opportunities that life offers. God bless you!

LORI & PAUL HOGAN
Co-Founders
Home Instead Senior Care

Introduction

A CARER'S STORY

In hindsight, the symptoms of Alzheimer's disease began for Dad much earlier than any of us were willing to admit. My first reactions were complete and total denial.

One day Mum called frantically to say Dad had gone out in the car to run errands, and still hadn't come home. Sure enough, he was lost and was trying to find his way home all day.

Slowly, I watched my dad get worse. The words seemed to slip away. He could not put together a full sentence. He could not button his shirt. He couldn't work the remote control and he started to talk about going "home" when he was already there with my mum.

I knew something was wrong, but I couldn't bear to think that my Dad could have Alzheimer's disease.

This was when I became sad and angry. I often woke up in the middle of the night, crying. I cried in the shower. I cried every time I left his flat. I missed him. I wanted to be able to talk to him and have him understand. I had many things going on in my life, which he would have been so excited about. I felt it was so unfair. This man did not deserve Alzheimer's disease. Does anyone?

One morning, as I lay in bed crying, it hit me. If he knew that people were caring for him, he would hate it. But no one deserved to be taken care of more. Maybe this was God's way of paying my father back for all the good he had done in his lifetime. I suddenly felt so much better. I realised that this was our chance. I knew that from here on in, it wasn't about being sad for my loss. It was going to be about providing him with the best care and the most dignity possible. It was going to be about taking care of Dad in the same loving way that he had taken care of so many people during his lifetime.

Jackie M.

When a person you know or love gets Alzheimer's disease or other dementias, everything changes. Devastating is the day when your most intimate friend or life partner no longer recognises you. Heartbreaking is the first time your well-educated and successful father can no longer remember how to brush his teeth. Frightening is the call from the corner shop that Mum is there and can't find her way home.

As a carer, you will likely struggle to understand the full impact of dementia; it's easy to become overwhelmed.

Despite years of research and a worldwide effort, there is still no cure for these diseases. Meanwhile according to Alzheimer's Society there are currently 800,000 people living with dementia in the UK, with that figure predicted to rise to over a million by 2021.

People generally want to stay in their home for as long as possible and people with dementia feel the same way. Their family carers also often desire to have them at home.

Alzheimer's Society reports that there are 670,000 carers of people living with dementia in the UK, and this guide has been designed as a quick and easy resource to help give you – the family carer – the confidence and skills you need to care for a parent, spouse, extended family member or friend with dementia at home.

OVERVIEW OF DEMENTIA

Dementia is a group of illnesses that affects memory and the ability to recall information. Dementia also leads to confusion, which affects personality and social behaviour. Dementia can impact judgment, thinking, behaviour, language and the ability to perform everyday tasks. There are many types of dementia, but the most common is Alzheimer's disease.

Dementia impacts all five senses. The diseases can affect field of vision and depth perception. What's more, the impact of ageing already may be taking a toll on those areas. The abilities to see and understand are at the core of dementia, so when hearing loss is also present, the person's condition is further challenged. The inability to see or hear adequately denies or distorts the processing of information by the already challenged brain.

The causes of dementia are not fully understood; however, most experts agree there are likely many factors at work. The greatest risk factor for dementia is growing older, but a progressive dementia, such as Alzheimer's disease, is NOT a normal part of ageing. Other risk factors may include family history, cardiovascular disease and a history of head trauma or concussions.

Some researchers think lifestyle could matter as much as family history. All of us may be able to lower the odds of developing a dementia or delaying its onset by exercising, eating well, staying socially active and embracing life-long learning. In other words, using our brains!

STAGES OF DEMENTIA

Most experts agree that dementia does progress in stages, but symptoms will vary greatly from person to person. Not everyone will experience the same symptoms or progress at the same rate.

People in the early stages of dementia are still functioning well and require minimal assistance and cues. They may have memory lapses and forget familiar words or become confused in familiar places. In the early stages, they may have trouble handling money, and experience mood or personality changes.

Symptoms in the middle stages become more pronounced and challenging for the family to handle. There is also an increase in memory loss and confusion. The person may have trouble recognising family and friends, repeat stories, and have difficulty carrying out tasks that have multiple steps.

The late stage of dementia is when full-time care is typically needed. This can be the most difficult stage for the family carer. The person with dementia may have lost the ability to recognise herself or her family, can no longer communicate and needs total assistance with personal care.

To ensure proper diagnosis, it's important to seek assistance from a medical professional. A complete check up can rule out treatable diseases, inform you about medications that could help a family member, and give you a better understanding of the disease. The earlier you acknowledge the symptoms, plan and get help, the better.

SYMPTOMS OF ALZHEIMER'S DISEASE AND DEMENTIA

According to Alzheimer's Society, the most common symptoms of Alzheimer's disease include:

- Struggling to remember recent events
- Finding it hard to follow conversations or programmes on television
- Forgetting the names of friends or everyday objects
- Inability to recall things that have been heard, seen or read
- Repetition or losing the thread in conversations
- Problems with thinking and reasoning
- Feelings of anxiety, depression or anger at forgetfulness
- Feeling confused even when in a familiar environment

If you've ever had a migraine headache, you know that it's not the disorder itself that causes havoc – it's the symptoms you have to live through that disrupt your day or night. People with migraines commonly experience blurred vision and strange smells, and/or have extreme pain and nausea. Similarly, it's the symptoms of dementia that create such an emotionally, physically and financially stressful experience for families. It can be helpful to think about **two categories** of symptoms: **memory** and **behaviour** symptoms.

Confusion is an example of a **memory** or cognitive symptom. If a person becomes confused about the day of the week, that may cause frustration for the one with dementia, but would result in no harm. However, if the confusion is causing that individual to forget to pay bills, it can result in serious issues or even make your family member vulnerable to scams.

An example of a **behaviour** symptom is wandering. Wandering away from home can have an unfortunate outcome. Some behavioural symptoms may put the safety of the person or others at risk, while others symptoms can be frustrating and difficult.

The following chart provides a general ranking of these behaviours in terms of frustration, difficulty and danger.

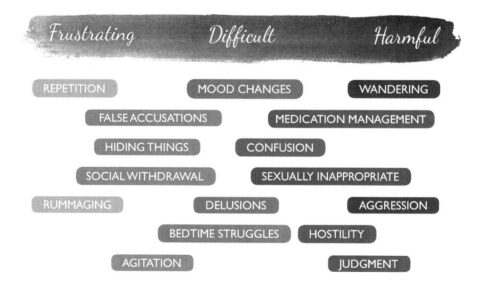

Frustrating	*Difficult*	*Harmful*
REPETITION	MOOD CHANGES	WANDERING
FALSE ACCUSATIONS	MEDICATION MANAGEMENT	
HIDING THINGS	CONFUSION	
SOCIAL WITHDRAWAL	SEXUALLY INAPPROPRIATE	
RUMMAGING	DELUSIONS	AGGRESSION
	BEDTIME STRUGGLES	HOSTILITY
AGITATION		JUDGMENT

This book will focus on both **memory** and **behaviour** symptoms that family carers often need help with, including common personal care activities. Each of these chapters will offer plenty of care approaches and prevention tips, and begin with a relevant and moving real-life family carer story. The chapters are as follows:

- Aggression and Anger
- Agitation and Anxiety
- Bedtime Struggles and Sleep Problems
- Confusion and Memory Loss
- Delusions
- False Accusations and Paranoia
- Hiding/Misplacing Things/Rummaging
- Hostility
- Judgment (problems with decision-making and problem-solving)
- Medication Mismanagement
- Mood Changes
- Repetition
- Sexually Inappropriate Behaviour
- Social Withdrawal
- Wandering

In general, behaviours usually arise when a person has an unmet need. Because language is often affected by dementia, people with this disease may "tell" you about their needs or issues by "showing" you. By acting in a certain way, they may be trying to communicate what they want or need. By "listening to what they do," it's possible to understand and manage that unmet need.

Quick Check: Are they. . . ?

If your family member exhibits any behavioural symptoms, using the list below may provide clues for you to offer effective support. When you consider how different each of us is, it's no surprise that there really isn't one, single, dementia experience.

EMOTIONAL
Bored
Sad
Tired
Embarrassed
Affectionate
Feeling Supported
Stressed
Afraid
Frustrated
Valued
Lacking Trust
Feeling Unsafe

SOCIAL
Unable to Talk
Feeling Left Out
Lacking Relationships
Accepting of Changes
Isolated
Bored
Lonely

PHYSICAL
Hot or Cold
Wearing Restricting Clothing
In Pain
Hungry
Thirsty
Sheltered

ENVIRONMENTAL
In a Noisy Room
In a Crowded Area
In New or Different Surroundings
Living with Clutter
Over-Stimulated
Living with Poor Lighting
Introduced to Strangers

APPROACHING CARE AT HOME

With dementia affecting the core cognitive functions of a person, providing care will not always be easy. One of the most crucial things to understand is that as a carer, you will have to make changes to maintain the person's quality of life, as well as your own.

Being present in their world, validating and reassuring the person, and serving and supporting are ways to ease the care situation. For example, when the person with dementia is talking about her mother, who is deceased, your role is to validate her feelings rather than bring her back to "reality" about her mother. By being in their moment, you will have a better opportunity for successful caregiving.

This may require you to tell a "therapeutic lie" or go along with the person in his or her confusion to avoid upsetting the situation. For example, if you are trying to get Dad to bathe and you know he used to be in the Army, you may encourage him to get into the shower because the "Major is coming by for an inspection in 30 minutes." By using this technique to smooth over a brief moment of confusion, you are helping long term. The result of poor hygiene would have negative effects on several areas of Dad's life, so convincing him to bathe is of the utmost importance.

It is also important to understand your family member's life story to help you with the caregiving experience. This allows you to personalise the care you give and engage that individual in a meaningful life. Knowing the person's life story also will help you with behavioural symptoms.

Putting the person and his or her needs at the centre of the caregiving experience is the key to this approach. When you try to provide care on your schedule or by your method, this may not always coincide with the person receiving care, which leads to frustration for both the individual and the carer. With the uncertainty of this disease, flexibility will be important.

You may already know a lot about your family member or close friend and just need to refresh your memory. Or, if it's an extended family member for whom you are caring, you may need to go on a fact-finding mission. Simple steps to take include:

- Asking the person questions
- Observing their surroundings, including knowing their routines
- Asking family members and friends questions

Recording this information is important so that you can review and refer back as needed. A journal, a notebook or your computer will suffice to keep the information.

Some common themes when gathering data include:

- Likes, Preferences and Routines
- Family
- Childhood
- Growing Up and Culture
- Adult Life
- Big Events

Your family member's "likes" along with his or her routines are important to honour as you provide care. Remembering if they prefer a bath rather than a shower can make this a smoother task. Or recalling that the person has a cup of tea every night before bed can make the bedtime ritual relaxed and less stressful.

Narrow down a short list of that person's life experiences, so if any agitation occurs, you can quickly turn to these themes for a possible solution.

TECHNIQUES

Here are the essential techniques to help you manage care at home.

REDIRECT

Redirect means "changing directions." Changing the topic or mood from bad to good and creating a more positive and safe result are the objectives.

For instance, if your family member asks or says the same thing over and over, such as, "What time is it?" or "I want to go home," you could use their personal information and redirect to a favourite subject or activity. The redirect technique is effective in managing many situations.

APOLOGISE AND TAKE THE BLAME

Apologising or taking the blame takes the attention off the person. The individual may calm down if he or she believes a situation was not their fault. Even when it isn't your fault, an apology sometimes solves the problem and allows you to regroup and move on to a more positive situation. It is often best to offer a simple apology, "I'm sorry I misunderstood you."

PHYSICALLY REMOVE THE PERSON OR CHANGE THE ENVIRONMENT

People can become agitated, upset or overly focused on something in their environment. For example, they may become upset because there are too many clothes in the wardrobe or want to use potentially dangerous power tools in the garage simply because they are in plain sight. Move distracting, disturbing or potentially harmful things out of the way and simplify the environment where possible.

GIVE SIMPLE CHOICES

Offering simple choices helps the person feel in control. Someone with dementia may feel he or she has no control over life. If the person refuses to do something and becomes angry, offering simple choices may help calm him or her and restore control. Asking, for example, "Would you like eggs or cereal for breakfast?" may work better than merely setting down a bowl of cornflakes.

ENGAGE IN MEANINGFUL ACTIVITIES

Research supports the importance of meaningful activities. Mental, physical and social activities can create positive emotional responses that diminish stress and anxiety for the person with dementia. Participating in activities helps the person feel a sense of purpose and accomplishment, even if it is as simple as answering a trivia question or making a successful trip to the grocery shop.

You may have to try various approaches and use these techniques multiple times. When you use one technique and do not have success, try it again in a few minutes using a different approach.

Do not get discouraged. This easy to follow book includes guidance on supportive approaches, proven techniques, and plenty of tips and strategies from experts and family carers like you. In the following chapters you will find specifics on how to react, and tips to try as you respond and communicate.

You won't have to read this guide from cover-to-cover to get what you need. Rather, go to the section that features information about the situation you're dealing with on a given day, and you'll find workable solutions to help make your life easier.

Before we delve into the alphabetised chapters of the most common issues that family carers face when caring for someone with dementia, we want to address the day-to-day personal care activities that could be becoming more difficult.

Personal Care Activities

Personal care activities are tasks that most of us take for granted, but ones that can be particularly difficult when a person has dementia. When your family member needs assistance with these types of activities, it also conveys the message that they are no longer able to care entirely for themselves.

This loss of independence can be very difficult to accept for both you and your family member. Personal care can be a complicated task for the person living with dementia because there are numerous steps and choices. The tasks of bathing, dressing, eating and using the toilet involve motor skills, adequate vision, sequencing, memory recall and decision-making.

At any support group or family meeting, one of the most talked about subjects is **bathing**. Those with dementia often resist bathing. Families may struggle to get a shower or bath accomplished and keep the person with dementia clean. Often Mum won't remember why she should be taking a bath, may be modest or shy about removing her clothes, have some discomfort or pain from arthritis, be afraid of falling or just simply resist.

Families often notice something is wrong with Mum and Dad when their appearance and **dressing** habits change. Mum, who had always been so neat and tidy, now is wearing the same stained blouse or has many layers of clothing on at one time. Dressing is a very personal and private activity for most of us. Many people have never dressed or undressed in front of another person and this can be an uncomfortable experience.

Eating and **drinking** habits may change with dementia. Some may want to eat all the time, or not at all. A declining sense of smell may affect the person's ability to taste. Getting Mum or Dad to drink enough liquids to stay hydrated may be a difficult task as well. As the disease progresses, even swallowing could become a problem. In that case, be sure to consult your doctor to get medical advice on how to safely prepare food. Mum may still try to use the cooker or prepare food on her own (which can become unsafe over time). Eventually she could lose the ability to make her own meals. These changes make ensuring a family member has the proper nutrition as the disease progresses a growing challenge.

Incontinence could also affect a person with dementia. For example, he could forget to go, not recognise the toilet, urinate in an inappropriate place or have trouble unfastening his trousers. There can be medical reasons for this, including urinary tract infections or side effects from medicines, but more often than not, incontinence comes from the decline in memory and thinking.

BEING THE CARER

Having to care for a parent or family member in these personal ways can be difficult physically and emotionally. Take time to adjust so that you are comfortable in this new role. Some people never become fully comfortable and feel guilty when they cannot do it. Read on to gain a better understanding to determine if this is a role meant for you.

When helping a family member with dementia through personal care activities, effective communication is the key. Remain calm, supportive and confident, keep an even tone of voice and use non-threatening body language. Encourage independence by letting Dad do as much as he can by assisting from a distance.

Go slowly and move at Dad's pace. If you appear annoyed, this may cause him to feel ashamed, depressed, anxious and embarrassed. Always try to reassure Dad and let him know you will protect his privacy during these personal activities. For example, cover him with a blanket while undressing or close the door and curtains in his room.

Another way to help preserve Mum's dignity is to have a familiar person, preferably of the same sex, assist with these activities. The following **care approaches** will offer ideas on how to navigate your journey through personal care. Employ some creativity as you ease into this role.

CARE APPROACHES

ROUTINES AND PREFERENCES

* Set a regular time for bathing. Do things the same way and at the same time each day. Change routines only when they're not working.

* Try to maintain his personal style. If Dad wore smart trousers and a shirt every day, asking him to wear jeans and t-shirts may confuse him.

* Continue food traditions for as long as possible. For example, make Grandma's pasta sauce and ask her to help. If she is unable, ask her to sit near and watch, assisting if she can.

* Have a routine for taking Mum to the bathroom and stick to it as closely as possible. For example, take her to the bathroom every three hours or so during the day. Don't wait for Mum to ask. Say, "Mum, the bathroom is down the hall. Let's go."

MODIFY AND SIMPLIFY THE TASK

* If you can't convince Dad to take a shower or a bath, try getting by with a sponge bath. Consider alternatives such as no-rinse bathing wipes and dry shampoo.

* Try breaking the task into simple, manageable steps and doing them one at a time. For example, "Step into the shower now." "Let's get your hair wet." "Put some soap in your hand." "Rub it on your hair." Reassure Mum each time she completes a step.

* If you need to cut Dad's food for him, do it out of his sight line to help preserve his dignity.

- Keep the table setting simple and avoid patterned dishes, placemats and tablecloths. Patterns can be confusing as vision worsens, or distracting when you need Mum to eat.

- Consider serving just one item of food at a time. For example, if you're having soup and sandwiches, serve the soup first and then the sandwich. Limit the number of utensils and serve small portions.

- Go with clothing and shoes that are easy to slip on, such as those with Velcro fasteners. Select fabrics that don't require ironing.

USE CONTRAST

- Look to create contrast on the dinner plate. Mum may not be able to see turkey, potatoes and cauliflower on a white plate. Consider a coloured plate.

- Depending on the colour of the bedspread, if you lay out clothes they may blend in. Either lay out a white sheet over the bedspread or hang clothes against a contrasting background.

SIMPLE CHOICES

- Give Mum choices. Ask, "Would you like to take a bath or a shower?" or "Do you want a bath now or after breakfast?"

- Offer a choice between a white shirt and a blue shirt.

- Ask, "Would you like to go out for lunch today, Dad, or stay in for leftovers?"

BE DESCRIPTIVE AND GIVE CUES

- Make sure to explain the task to Mum before beginning to help reduce confusion. For instance, "Mum, first I will blow dry your hair on low heat. Then we will put in some of your favourite hair slides."

- Continue to give details of the task while it's happening, using short, simple, but descriptive words. "Grandpa, take your comb and run it through your hair."

- If Dad doesn't recognise what he is eating, describe each item on his plate.

- Use familiar and respectful words to describe objects and actions.

- For example, refer to incontinence products as underpants and knickers rather than incontinence pads.

- Cueing or reminding may help the person to dress independently. "Dad, it's almost time for church. Shall we start to get dressed?" Or say, "Mum, I need to go to the toilet. Do you need to go as well?"

- Lay out articles of clothing in sequence on the bed. They should be arranged in the order that they are meant to be put on.

- Use helpful language. For example, "Dinner is in a few minutes. Will you help me set the table?"

- Tap into Mum's life story to plan activities that would cue her to want to shower and change clothes. For example, getting dirt on her trousers after gardening may help convince her to shower and put on clean clothes.

CREATE PLEASANT DIVERSIONS AND REWARDS

- Start the bath time with something Mum enjoys, such as having her back washed. She then may allow you to assist with other areas.

- Create a spa-like atmosphere at bath time. Buy Mum's favourite lavender soaps and lotions to help create a pleasing experience.

- Setting the mood in advance will make for a more pleasant experience for you and your family member. Try soothing music.

- Offering a reward may help convince her to get in the shower. "After you shower, Mum, we will go to the park to feed the ducks." Or "Mum, once you finish eating dinner, let's pop out for an ice cream."

- Offer praise when a task has been completed successfully. That helps build self-esteem. For example, "Grandma, you look great today. Wonderful job picking out that beautiful sweater."

THREE TIMES, THREE WAYS

- If you're having trouble convincing your spouse to take a shower, first say, "Darling, it's time for a shower." If he resists, try a second time and say, "If you shower now, you'll be done just in time to read the morning paper." Finally, if he continues to resist, schedule an event. Say, "Sweetheart, church is today. Remember, you always like to shower before church."

- If Mum doesn't want to eat lunch, first say, "Mum, breakfast was four hours ago. Is your tummy growling?" Next, try, "Mum, you didn't eat much at breakfast, so let's have lunch. You need a good meal so you have energy for our walk later." A third try could be, "Mum, we are having your favourite chicken salad sandwiches for lunch. Come and eat."

MODEL

- If Mum is unsure what to do with her utensils, show her by picking up your spoon to eat the dessert. If that doesn't work, put the spoon in her hand and guide her hand to her mouth.

- Instead of brushing the crumbs off Grandpa's shirt, pretend you're brushing crumbs off your shirt, hoping he will follow your lead.

- If Mum is not drinking enough liquids, try enticing her by saying, "Gosh, I'm thirsty, Mum. A glass of squash sounds good." Or, "My mouth is really dry. I could use some squash."

- If you are assisting with tooth brushing, ask Dad to stand in front of a mirror while you help from behind, so he can still see what he's doing.

APOLOGISE, TAKE THE BLAME

- If Dad becomes frustrated during dinner because he can't chew his food, apologise and take the blame. "I'm sorry that I served you this tough piece of meat, Dad. I should have cooked it better."

- To ease embarrassment of an accident, blame it on an external factor. For example, "Mum, I am sorry about your accident. Next time I will buy trousers with fewer buttons."

PREVENTION

Flexibility and the opportunity to adapt are the "name of the game" when caring for a family member with dementia. Planning for success as well as looking ahead could help you avoid frustration and save time. Writing down observations about a family member's daily routine may help you identify triggers that could lead to fewer accidents and frustrations. By trying these ideas below, you can learn to be proactive with your approaches to care.

PLAN AHEAD

- When it's bath time, gather all supplies including soft towels, scented soaps and shampoo. Baby shampoo, which won't sting Mum's eyes, is a good option. Remove clutter and make sure the path to the bathroom is clear. Set out everything you need – towels, washcloths, soap, shampoo, fresh clothes – and then just gently lead Mum to the shower and talk her through the process, assisting when needed.

- Make sure the bath or shower water is not too hot or too cold. Pay attention to the temperature in the room as well, to ensure that Mum is comfortable.

- Leave the bathroom door open and the toilet seat up when not in use so it is obvious that the toilet is vacant.

- At mealtimes, use a plastic tablecloth or placemats for easier clean-up. Ask Mum to wear an apron to protect her clothing.

- Include finger foods on your daily menu such as small sandwiches, and sliced fruits and vegetables.

- If Dad is incontinent, safeguard mattresses and furniture with protective covers. This will help when cleaning up.

- Try replacing underwear in his drawers with disposable briefs.

- When preparing for an outing with Grandpa, know in advance where the toilets are located. Get him to wear simple, easy-to-remove clothing and take along an extra set in case of an accident.

- Group Mum's clothes into outfits. When she can grab one hanger with a skirt and a shirt, she will feel confident in her selection.

KEEP A JOURNAL

- Watch for any signs that Dad may need to go to the bathroom, such as fidgeting, restlessness, hiding behind furniture or pulling at his clothes.

- Understanding when, where and why accidents happen can help you avoid them. Writing down these triggers could also help.

- Record any possible irritants for Mum such as coffee, alcohol, or fizzy drinks.

- Notice and record changes in Grandma's appetite. Keep a food diary, including spices and other details of items that could irritate her digestion.

- Observe the time of day when your spouse has the most energy and schedule the more complicated tasks, such as bathing, at that time.

ADAPT

* A shower chair can help if Mum's mobility is limited and she has trouble standing. Add grab bars in the shower.

* For some people, buttons, poppers, hooks, zips and belt buckles are too difficult to manage. Try replacing with Velcro fasteners – they're easier for you and Dad.

* Slip-on shoes can help Dad continue to complete this task on his own. Make sure shoes have non-skid soles.

* Select clothing that is washable and doesn't need ironing.

* Mum may lose her taste for what she once loved, or develop other food preferences. Have a variety of healthy snacks and other options on hand for her.

* Adapt tableware. Use a bowl, for instance, instead of a plate to make eating easier. Cups with lids and straws will help ensure fewer spills.

THINK CREATIVELY

* Ask for Mum's help trying out a new soap or lotion.

* If you're struggling to convince Dad to get dressed, present him with a gift. Wrap up new or even existing clothing. When he opens the present, ask him to try it on to see if it fits.

* If your spouse is wearing the same outfit day after day, know that it is not uncommon. Rather than trying to reason with him to change, it's often better to buy a few of the same outfits so you can have some of his favourite ensembles clean and ready to go at all times.

* If Grandma is having trouble with her bowels and digestion, offer her fibre-rich foods such as apples or green vegetables.

- If Dad isn't eating, turn mealtime into an event. For example, plan a family dinner gathering just because it's the weekend!

- If Mum has lost the ability to use wardrobes and drawers, hang clean clothes on doorknobs, scatter clean socks and underwear around the room, and keep shoes in plain sight.

DOCTOR'S ORDERS

- Routine dental checkups and daily oral health care to keep the mouth and teeth healthy will be important. Make sure dentures fit properly.

- Regular eye tests and having his glasses checked will help keep Dad independent for longer.

- Talk with her doctors. They can advise about the best ways to get adequate nutrition, including when to use supplements like nutritional supplement drinks. In addition, there are a number of medications on the market for urinary incontinence.

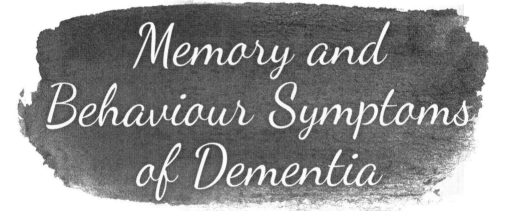

Memory and Behaviour Symptoms of Dementia

AGGRESSION AND ANGER

This senior had been having problems misplacing items of importance such as his wallet, keys, money and TV remote. He kept trying to borrow ladders from his neighbour as he was convinced that the items were on the roof of his house and he wished to climb up onto the roof to retrieve them.

When not allowed onto the roof for his keys he became very agitated and angry with anyone who was around. This man suffered from hallucinations and these were made worse when he became agitated. In order to calm the situation down, we would redirect the client to activites that would reduce his anger and agitation.

This senior had spent time in the Navy and on the Tall Ships in Liverpool. We found that anything to do with water such as filling a bowl made him happy and calmed the situation down.

— Melanie F.

WHY DOES THIS HAPPEN?

There's nothing more difficult or unsettling than seeing someone become angry or aggressive, especially when you're trying to help and keep them safe. Aggression is a verbal or physical lashing out toward another person.

People with dementia may become angry for a variety of reasons. A person with this disease who becomes angry has many frustrations because of things that were once easy he can no longer do and because they are confused. Because this client's brain isn't functioning normally, the one way he can communicate his wishes is through aggression. The clear message from him: "Stop what you are doing!"

For example, if you stop putting up the ladders – as Melanie found – and he doesn't understand your intent, he is going to try to stop you with his words and sometimes with actions.

Your approach is important in restoring calm. So are certain strategies and techniques, such as the ones Liza used. You may feel afraid, threatened or shocked by the aggression, but you can gain confidence and success with changes to your approach.

(Emotional • Social • Physical • Environmental)

Does the person have an unmet need that is causing the memory or behavioural symptom?

CARE APPROACHES

* When Mum or Dad is angry, arguing with them may escalate the situation. Validate their feelings and try to gain understanding so you can restore order.

- Give Dad what he wants as long as it's not dangerous. Apologise and even take the blame to help defuse the situation.

- Stay calm. Because you had good intentions, you may feel afraid or shocked by the aggression, but try not to express this through your body language. Let your face show genuine concern.

- Try to keep your voice tone even and polite. Grandpa is still an adult and if you try to boss him, this could be insulting.

- Check your body posture. Keep your hands at your sides or, if seated, in your lap. Stand or sit at the same level as Dad so that your relationship is equal. If you have backed off, wait for an invitation to approach.

- Slow down! Mum may need time to adjust to your physical presence in the room, and if you are rushed, she will become more confused.

- Make sure Mum sees or hears you before you touch her, so try rustling some papers or softly clear your throat. Make eye contact with Mum. An unexpected approach and touch could be very upsetting to her.

- Greet her by name and perhaps talk about the weather or the picture on her wall.

- Step back out of harm's way (even leave the room for a few minutes if necessary) and take a few deep breaths. Sometimes simply letting things cool down works wonders.

- Be sensitive to privacy. The person with dementia may be uncomfortable during care tasks like bathing, dressing and toileting. Always have a towel, or clothing within reach to offer your family member. Or even consider looking away to help them feel more comfortable.

- Create moments of pleasure before beginning a task. Your spouse might be much more willing to get dressed in the morning after a refreshing cup of coffee or tea and a slice of toast.

- When it's time to help Mum dress, realise she may not see a need for changing her clothes. Appeal to her vanity and give her a reason, like telling her she will want to look nice for her visitors.

- Sometimes "bribery" works. For instance, after a bath promise a cup of cocoa or a snack.

- Give simple choices. Instead of asking Dad to wear a clean shirt, give him the choice between the blue shirt or the yellow shirt.

- If there are several people in the kitchen, for example, have the carer Mum trusts most stay with her. Ask all others to withdraw.

- Remove valuable and breakable objects. You wouldn't want a family heirloom to become broken or damaged.

- Once a person who is upset begins to calm down, refer to their life story to redirect to a more enjoyable activity such as:

  — A walk

  — Soothing music

  — Painting a picture

  — Watching a video

  — A useful job such as washing dishes or potting a plant

  — Mixing, measuring and pouring ingredients for a favourite recipe

STARTING THE CONVERSATION

When communicating with a person who is angry, tone of voice, volume, pace and inflection are crucial for the conversation as well as speaking with confidence and using supportive language. When you offer simple choices or take the blame, you are validating feelings and reassuring the individual with dementia.

"I'm here for you, Dad. We will get through this together. The nice, hot shower will be over before you know it."

"Dad, I know you're frustrated that you can't remember the date today. This must be hard for you."

"I am sorry that I upset you," or "I didn't mean to upset you; I was just trying to help."

"Hey, I've become pretty good at making the bed. Let me help you out."

"I can see you are uncomfortable in that sweater. Let me get you a different one."

"Do you want to brush your teeth first or wash your face?"

"Mum, once you are finished in the bathroom, I will get you a hot chocolate before bed."

PREVENTION

Following are tips to consider to help prevent these actions from occurring again.

- **LEARN WHAT UPSETS YOUR DAD BY INVOLVING THE WHOLE FAMILY IF NECESSARY AND CREATE A JOURNAL.** It shouldn't take much detective work to discover when angry and aggressive actions occur. Understand when/where/why the angry episode occurred (for example, TV show, neighbour visiting, reminder of something in the past) and avoid these situations in the future. Refer to this journal often and update it as the disease progresses.

- **LOOK FOR WAYS TO SIMPLIFY TASKS.** People often become frustrated and then angry by being unable to complete simple tasks they used to do easily like buttoning a shirt or tying shoelaces. Substitute pull-on polo shirts with fewer buttons or a front fastening zip and slip-on or Velcro fastening shoes.

AGITATION AND ANXIETY

Dad would get that look in his eyes: Nobody's home. His eyes would glaze over and he'd get more dazed and agitated. We didn't get it then, but having him deal with crowds was a trigger.

For example, we'd take him Christmas shopping, and he'd kick at the displays. So we now avoid situations with large crowds. One time, we were all standing in the kitchen making dinner and he came in and acted like we were all in a scrum. Because Dad was a rugby coach in his younger days, he started giving instructions. By letting him go with his past memory, his mood began to lighten. Later that night, he just sat alone staring at the fire for hours, so calm. He seemed like he was having a nice, quiet time.

— Tessa S.

WHY DOES THIS HAPPEN?

Dad's agitation and anxiety can upset the entire family. Anxiety is experiencing worry, uneasiness or nervousness, while agitation is the physical result of that anxiety. Dad may be restless, fidgety, unable to sleep well, unable to concentrate on tasks and may pace (walk to the point of exhaustion).

With Tessa's father, large crowds were the trigger to the anxiety and agitation. With others, it could be the seemingly smallest things, such as a book out of place.

When Tessa's family understood Dad's trigger, they knew how to respond. You can do the same when you understand what's causing agitation and anxiety with your family member.

(Emotional • Social • Physical • Environmental)

Does the person have an unmet need that is causing the memory or behavioural symptom?

CARE APPROACHES

* Anxiety often comes from an environment that is too stimulating or too boring. Try de-cluttering work surfaces in the kitchen or brightening the kitchen table with flowers from the garden.

* Frustration and agitation may come from noise or glare from TV or loud music. Learn Dad's trigger point and avoid it in the future.

* Create a calm space for Mum to go to when she is upset. Make sure she recognises her favourite things in this place, such as her favourite seat in the garden, surrounded by the flowers she planted.

- Be aware of what's in Mum's line of vision. Sit in her favourite chair. Is the flickering TV screen, which changes at least every few seconds, upsetting her?

- Make sure Grandma has enough light for reading by her favourite chair. Low lighting could trigger agitation and anxiety.

- Create a change of scenery. Rather than serving your spouse lunch in front of the television, where he sits most of the day, serve lunch at the kitchen table.

- Try a gentle touch. Many love having their hands held, an arm stroked, or a back rubbed. Know what pleases Mum and provide it.

- Your loving voice can provide much comfort when your family member is agitated. Long after a person forgets your name, he or she will react to the familiar sound of your voice.

- Knowing Dad's preferences and routines can make a big difference. For example, if Dad prefers a bath rather than a shower, make sure to accommodate this to avoid upsetting him.

- Refocus the person's attention. If your spouse is anxious about an upcoming doctor's appointment that is hours or even days away, assure her that you will get there in time. For now, redirect her to an activity such as gardening or painting. Food and drink can be great distractors, too.

- When Mum is anxious, try offering comfort from a beloved family pet or grandchildren. Look at a picture book.

- Fresh air and nature can have a positive impact. Go outdoors for a walk whenever possible, preferably in your favourite park.

- Everybody likes a good laugh. Show a funny YouTube video or read jokes from a joke book to ease her agitation.

- Give Mum a chance to feel useful. Get her to do simple tasks such as sweeping a path or folding the laundry.

- Providing something familiar can be calming. Some women may hang onto handbags or spoons. Some men may like to jingle coins or keys in a pocket, or keep a newspaper under an arm.

- If your family member is pacing, ask if you could join in the walk. From there look for an opportunity to suggest you both sit down.

- If Mum gets easily flustered when faced with decisions, simplify her choices. Ask Mum if she would like to have porridge or toast for breakfast, two of her favourites.

- Be prepared. If Dad has low blood sugar and you are going for a long doctor's appointment, be sure to take healthy snacks.

STARTING THE CONVERSATION

Your body language can have a big impact on the situation. If you're relaxed and calm, this will show in your face, posture and the tone of your voice. When you empathise with how your mother is feeling, she will calm down from the reassurance.

"We'll get to the doctor's appointment in time, Mum.
How about a cup of tea first?"

. . . .

"I can see you're concerned about the pile of papers and
I am too. Let me clean that up."

. . . .

"I know you're missing your mother. Tell me your favourite
story about her."

. . . .

"Mother Teresa was a great woman. What did you
like best about her?"

. . . .

"Mum, I know that summer is your favourite time of year.
Do you know tomorrow is the first day of summer? Let's make
a list of some fun things to do when it gets hot."

. . . .

"I can only imagine how hard this must be for you;
but I'm here, and I'll stick with you."

. . . .

"I am sorry that I upset you. Let's listen to some music
and try to take the bath later."

. . . .

"Dad, would you like milk or fruit juice with your dinner?"

PREVENTION

Following are tips to consider to help prevent these actions from occurring again.

- **WORK AS A FAMILY TO COME UP WITH SOLUTIONS.** For example, try visiting in pairs or at different times of the day to help minimise anxiety. Determine potential solutions together.

- **KEEP A FOOD DIARY.** Caffeine and sugar intake could be affecting Dad's agitation and anxiety.

- **PLAN AHEAD AND DON'T OVER-SCHEDULE.** Be sensitive to your spouse's most alert and most tired times of day and plan accordingly.

- **OBSERVE PATTERNS IN MUM'S BEHAVIOUR.** For example, if Mum always cooked dinner at 5 p.m., engage her in mealtime activities at that time of day to help prevent agitation.

BEDTIME STRUGGLES AND SLEEP PROBLEMS

My dad would get up, he'd turn on the light and that would wake my Mum up. She'd try to get him back to bed and then he'd say that he was hungry. That would go on for 20 or 30 minutes and then finally she'd get him back to bed and an hour later it would start all over again.

If he didn't turn on the light, she wouldn't wake up and he would wander out of the room. Then he wouldn't know where he was and he'd shout for her. So she'd wake up with her heart pounding, wondering what had happened and where he was.

Mum was so embarrassed, she wouldn't tell us what was going on, but things got better when she reached out for help.

— Debbie O.

WHY DOES THIS HAPPEN?

Nighttime can be challenging and even more so for carers like Debbie and her family. We all tend to wear out by the end of the day, but you may notice that Dad's symptoms can appear to worsen in the late afternoon and evenings. People with dementia might also confuse day and nighttime, causing sleep disturbances.

Be sure the person has been evaluated by a doctor for the common causes of sleep disturbances that often come with age, such as sleep apnea, restless leg syndrome and side effects of medications.

Also, reflect on your family member's day. If he's not sleeping at night, it could be because he is sleeping all afternoon. Finding meaningful activities throughout the day can help prevent excessive cat napping.

Remember, when the person isn't sleeping, neither is the carer; none of us can continue to be successful carers without enough sleep. Be sure to reach out like Debbie's mother did, before exhaustion sets in.

(Emotional • Social • Physical • Environmental)

Does the person have an unmet need that is causing the memory or behavioural symptom?

CARE APPROACHES

* Try encouraging your family member to get up a little earlier each day. The longer he is awake and engaged, the more likely a sound night's sleep will result.

* Engage Mum in physical activities such as gardening, walking and helping with housework. Even light exercise or walking around the local shopping centre can help ensure Mum is comfortably tired at bedtime.

- By providing adequate fluids to your family member, you decrease the risks of nighttime leg cramps and other discomforts.

- To avoid Dad feeling overly full and uncomfortable in the evening – which could keep him from a sound sleep – serve the last meal in the early evening and watch portion sizes.

- Tune into what Mum is reading and viewing. Limit the news, because stories about car accidents and bombings may cause a person with dementia to dream and even obsess about these terrible things.

- Understand Dad's sleep preferences and accommodate. If Dad always had a night light, keep one going in his room. If he doesn't like a lot of covers, make sure the room is warm.

- Check out things from Mum's point of view. Lie on the bed. Does a bright light shine in through the window all night? Does a mirror reflect light and cause shadows that could be alarming to her?

- Make sure the mattress is comfortable and the bedding is inviting. Does the mattress provide support without being too hard? Does your spouse have a favourite quilt, blanket or pillow?

- If bathing is what Mum always did at night, it's okay to modify this task with a quick face and hand wash before bed. That's easier for everyone.

- Wind down at the end of the day with simple tasks such as winding wool or looking through a picture book of favourite things. Continue to redirect the person to nighttime routines and activities.

- Build excitement for the next day. Keep a chalk board in a place where your spouse can see it. Put the day and the date, and a list of what you will be doing, noting that a good night's rest will be needed.

- Make bedtime a pleasant experience. Offer a foot, hand or backrub.

- Tuck Mum in with a hug and a kiss.

- Provide a favourite soothing and familiar piece of classical music or a lullaby.

- Tell a favourite story from Mum's childhood or recite a popular prayer.

- Install rope lighting on skirting boards or small night lights from Dad's room to the bathroom to guide him. This may help ease confusion when Dad is looking for the bathroom in the middle of the night.

STARTING THE CONVERSATION

Comforting phrases can help set the mood for bedtime. You can help ease Mum's bedtime anxieties by planning ahead, cueing appropriate activities at the right times and providing comforting touches.

"Here's the bathroom, Mum. You head in and I'll wait for you."

. . . .

If it's bedtime, say: "I'm really tired. You must be, too. Let's go to bed now."

. . . .

"Why don't we dim the lights, turn down the TV and read a bit before bedtime."

. . . .

"We did a lot of work in the garden today and need to get some rest."

. . . .

"We're going out tomorrow to have coffee with your best friend, so we need to get to bed now."

. . . .

"Why don't I rub this nice, warm lotion onto your hands, Dad."

. . . .

"Would you like hot milk or a cup of tea before bed?"

PREVENTION

Following are tips to consider to help prevent these actions from occurring again.

- **TRY TO DEVELOP A SLEEP SCHEDULE.** Sticking to the same bedtime and getting up at the same time each day can help with sleep issues. Even schedule a 30-minute nap after lunch each day if necessary. This could help you and Dad.

- **UNDERSTAND YOUR SPOUSE'S MEDICATIONS AND THE POSSIBLE EFFECTS ON SLEEP.** Some medications can cause either drowsiness or excitability.

- **LIMIT CAFFEINE.** Determine if any of Mum's foods have caffeine. Offer caffeine-free drinks to avoid keeping Mum up at night.

- **CONSIDER SAFETY PRECAUTIONS TO ENSURE YOUR PEACE OF MIND AND A RESTFUL SLEEP.** A monitor can alert you if Mum wakes up. If she is at risk of wandering, alarms are available for doors and windows, as well as specially designed locks.

CONFUSION AND
MEMORY LOSS

It's a new day every fifteen minutes for Mum. She's at the point now that, by the time you can finish your second sentence, she's asking you the question you were answering in your first sentence again. She tells stories from the past, but she recasts the players.

She had lung cancer two years ago and is in remission, but she'll still say things like, "When I get over this cancer ..."

We do not argue with her when she says something wrong. We just leave it alone because she's not hurting anyone.

— Sharon S.

WHY DOES THIS HAPPEN?

Confusion is one of the primary symptoms of dementia. Confusion tends to affect Mum's personality and social behaviour, whereas memory loss affects her ability to recall. Just like Sharon's mother, those with dementia confuse past and present, and cannot always reason things out.

Memory loss is what initiates the confusion. While you can't fix it, you can do important things to help your family member work around some of these problems. It is important that everyone understands these symptoms and develops consistent strategies that support Mum.

The confusion impacts the whole family, since it makes it harder to communicate and get everyday tasks accomplished. She may say, "I need the thing with the handle, the thing for my head." This could mean she wants her hairbrush. Or, she may struggle for the right word and come up with something close, like "my push" instead of "my brush."

Remember that the person with dementia always makes sense to herself. It's up to us to work out the message. By understanding some of the basic problems Mum is dealing with, you can organise your approach and the environment to reduce stress and help her be more self-sufficient.

(Emotional • Social • Physical • Environmental)

Does the person have an unmet need that is causing the memory or behavioural symptom?

CARE APPROACHES

* Don't argue with Mum if she's wrong. If she thinks you are her sister instead of her daughter, just go with it. Reassure her that she is loved and well-cared for.

- Be more descriptive in your explanations. Describe the day in simpler terms. Instead of saying its 7 a.m., explain that it's breakfast time or morning.

- Speak simply with short sentences, without being condescending.

- Avoid unnecessary details in daily conversation.

- Learn to be a creative listener. If you are having problems understanding what he is trying to say, listen closely. If you still can't understand, apologise and ask him to repeat.

- Confusion can cause Mum to misidentify certain articles. For example, she may be confused about what to do with a spoon. Start by demonstrating and lifting the spoon to your own mouth.

- Break down daily tasks such as dressing into simple steps. Lay out clothing for the day with the underwear on top of his clothes so that is the first thing he puts on.

- When Mum is confused by daily tasks, use the "your hand under their hand" technique to guide her through a task such as washing hair.

- Simplify the space to help Grandad succeed. In the bathroom, for example, clear the shelves. Then lay out just the towel, face cloth and a measured amount of shower gel or soap.

- Visual cues can help support your point. If you want to talk to Mum about the dress that she will be wearing to the wedding, get it out of the closet and show her.

- Be sure to use elements of her life story to provide cues, such as offering her a favourite drink, singing familiar songs or practicing past routines. Or redirect to a meaningful activity, such as helping you prepare dinner. This can help her feel more anchored to the day and less confused.

- Undertake activities in rooms that are smaller and quiet. If you're crafting with Mum, leave the distractions of the living room and go to a corner of the dining room where she can focus.

- Reduce the "extra" noise in the home. Having the TV on while the family is chatting or eating dinner should be avoided. The unnecessary extra stimuli could cause confusion.

- Engage Mum in activities that will help keep her mind active, such as word games, puzzles and trivia.

- Allow enough time. If you ask Dad if he prefers to go for a walk or read the paper, give him time to answer. Dad's brain impairment may force him to process information more slowly.

- Changes to Dad's day may increase confusion, so try to keep them to a minimum. If the washing machine breaks down, schedule the repairman during Dad's naptime to minimise confusion.

STARTING THE CONVERSATION

Confusion is at the heart of dementia. It impacts every area of a person's life. It's common for people to get distracted, lose one's train of thought, misidentify objects and be unable to retrieve words. So your ability to communicate is key. Limit input, learn to be a patient, good, creative listener, use visual cues, and demonstrate and simplify to help Mum understand and preserve her dignity.

If Mum says, "I'm waiting for Dad to pick me up," and Dad is deceased, say: "Tell me again about how you and Dad first met."

. . . .

If Dad says, "We just sold the car last week," but it's been five years, say: "I hope the new owner still loves the car as much as we did."

. . . .

Don't say, "We took Charlie the dog to the vet today for his injections and annual check-up," say "Charlie saw the dog doctor. He's feeling great!"

. . . .

Say: "Good morning! It's time for breakfast," instead of "It's 7 a.m. Get up."

. . . .

Say: "Let's brush your teeth, Dad, with the toothbrush." If he is confused, say: "Your toothbrush is in the cup next to the sink." If he is still confused say, "Let's brush together." (Hold the brush up to your mouth and make the brushing motion.)

. . . .

If Mum is confused about the task of folding towels say, "I'm sorry, Mum. I shouldn't have asked you to fold the towels when I knew you were tired."

. . . .

Say, "Dad, it's time for your usual cup of tea before bed."

PREVENTION

Following are tips to consider to help prevent these actions from occurring again.

- **IT'S GOOD TO OCCASIONALLY PAUSE AND THINK ABOUT THE IMPACT OF DEMENTIA ON DAD'S LIFE.** Put yourself in his shoes. What has his life been like and what has he lost?

- **MAINTAIN AN ORGANISED HOME FREE OF CLUTTER.** Keep the wardrobe tidy and group outfits to help Dad make easy selections and remain independent.

- **KEEP A JOURNAL WITH TRIGGERS FOR MUM'S CONFUSION.** It's hard to plan for unexpected disruptions, but maintaining a daily log could help you understand what prompts confusion.

DELUSIONS

A senior was determined that there was somebody in the upstairs of his house and that he was being burgled. Previous carers and family members had tried to reassure him by saying to him that there wasn't anyone there, i.e. don't be silly. As a result, because nobody believed him, he started not to trust, wouldn't let anyone into his house and cut himself off completely.

His care team knew it was important to gain his trust so they accompanied him upstairs and said "Let's go and see what they have taken and make sure they can't get back in."

When they all agreed that nothing was missing and all the windows were secure within a very short time he had forgotten all about it.

— Jackie R.

WHY DOES THIS HAPPEN?

If this gentleman is insisting that there are strangers in the house, he may be experiencing a delusion – a fixed, false idea.

There are a variety of potential causes for this condition including changes in the brain that occur as a result of dementia. While these issues can be frightening for the entire family there are strategies and techniques that can provide a solution for the family carer.

As the care team and family discovered, reacting calmly can help defuse the situation and preserve a person's dignity.

(Emotional • Social • Physical • Environmental)

Does the person have an unmet need that is causing the memory or behavioural symptom?

CARE APPROACHES

* In any occurrence react calmly, don't argue or try to reason or deny the experience. Reassure your family member that you are there with her and will help.

* Enter her reality. If Mum believes she is a young mother with toddlers, go along with her reality in a non-committal way by discussing how toddlers can be difficult. Redirect Mum to a favourite activity such as baking a cake.

* Understand Dad's triggers for delusions. For example, if he watched a violent TV show, he could think the bad guys are in the house. Turn the channel or redirect to a reading activity.

- If Dad says he is seeing strange lights, it may be an eye condition associated with ageing. Be sure to have his eyesight and hearing checked regularly.

- Check the environment for inadequate lighting, shadows, reflections and glare. These may trigger delusions in a person with dementia.

- If Mum is concerned that her food tastes differently or has gone off, take a step back and consider that certain medications may have caused her taste buds to change. Try to eat with Mum regularly to address her concerns.

- Helping Mum stay connected to the areas in life that she knew and loved could help minimise delusions. For example, if Mum was a housewife, keeping her engaged making dinner each night could help her stay in touch with the reality she once knew.

- If your spouse needs to move to a care home, take along pictures, furnishings, plants, etc., that can help him feel more at home and avoid confusion and delusions.

STARTING THE CONVERSATION

The biggest challenge of dealing with a delusion is to want to dismiss or correct it and bring the person back to reality. As long as the delusion is not causing harm, don't argue or try to reason or deny, just go with it. Redirect to a meaningful activity or physically remove the person from the situation.

If Mum says, "There's a man outside," say "He's just passing by. Let's go and have some lunch."

. . . .

"Mum, tell me more about what you see outside. Let's go and sit down and discuss this over tea."

. . . .

"Would it help if I sat with you? May I hold your hand?"

. . . .

If Dad sees a cat in his bed, say: "Let's sit in the living room and I will get Billy to take it outside."

. . . .

"I see how this is scary for you. I am here with you, Grandpa."

. . . .

She may say, "My mother (deceased) came to visit today." Say: "I'm sure you had a wonderful visit!"

PREVENTION

Following are tips to consider to help prevent these actions from occurring again.

- **TO UNDERSTAND WHY A DELUSION IS OCCURRING, SEEK A DOCTOR'S OPINION.** This will determine if the cause is, for example, a medication reaction or brain damage.

- **BE OBSERVANT.** Look for signs of bladder infection, constipation, skin changes, thirst, weight loss, sudden sleeplessness or heightened anxiety. Keep a journal to track anything that may cause a delusion.

- **INVOLVE FAMILY AND FRIENDS TO HELP COME UP WITH CREATIVE SOLUTIONS.** Remember, you're not in this alone. Identify those with skills to best support her and involve them in her care.

FALSE ACCUSATIONS AND PARANOIA

With Mum, this journey has had its ups and downs. Sometimes she is lucid and she can say how scary this is for her. Other times she just gets cross. She's suspicious we're trying to run her life. For whatever reason, she would become attached to grocery bags, for example. I've been thrown out of the room for trying to recycle them.

What we do is, we'll pick a room and say, "Hey, Mum, let's reorganise this room." We'll get her to tell stories about the things we find. Little by little, we're making some progress. But sometimes we'll be halfway through and she'll ask, "Why are you taking my things?" When that happens, we have to stop, right there, and change direction.

— Mary M.

WHY DOES THIS HAPPEN?

Imagine what it would be like to not know what is happening around you. Or what if you couldn't recognise everyone in your life?

Paranoia is a condition that develops, partly through fear, as the symptoms of dementia set in. As Mum loses the ability to recognise family, friends or home, a struggle develops within her to make sense of it and hold on to things, places and people.

That's why Mary's mother became paranoid and accused the family of taking her things when all they were doing was organising and recycling.

(Emotional • Social • Physical • Environmental)

Does the person have an unmet need that is causing the memory or behavioural symptom?

CARE APPROACHES

* Redirect Dad to a game of gin rummy or try to interest him in a walk to the park to see the ducks.

* If Mum accuses you of moving her favourite vase, even if you didn't do that, calmly apologise and take the blame. Reassure her and try to change the subject.

* If someone else is accused, stay calm and look for an opportunity to change the subject. When you have the opportunity, take the accused person aside and explain the situation while Mum is distracted.

* Keep Mum's close friends up to date about her situation so that during social outings they won't show concern.

- Provide your family member with a small amount of money to keep in her purse if she is used to having some money on hand.

- If your spouse wants to carry around an old pair of keys because he thinks they are his car keys, go with it. It may comfort him or he may feel he is keeping things safe.

- As the disease progresses, it's so important to keep the environment familiar. If you need to make a change in his living arrangement or environment, make sure he is always surrounded by the things that he loves and recognises.

- Designate an area in the home where Mum's favourite personal items are accessible, and label them.

- To avoid Dad losing his glasses, keep the house tidy. A clean environment will help make keeping track of items more efficient.

- Paranoia comes from fear and confusion. If she needs to buy a new dress, take her to the shops in the morning when there are fewer crowds.

- Get spare sets of important items for him, such as glasses or hearing aids. This will make replacement faster and easier.

- Try to redirect your family member if he or she is feeling suspicious or nervous. If Dad loves watching sports, get him to help you prepare a tray of cakes and biscuits for you both to enjoy while watching the match.

- Before discounting Mum's accusation, check out the facts. After all, older adults can be easy targets for scams.

STARTING THE CONVERSATION

If Mum is accusing you of something she thinks you've done or taken, the natural reaction will be to get defensive. The disease is robbing Mum of her life and this might be a way she is trying to exert some control. Don't take it personally. Reassure and validate her feelings, and encourage positive thoughts. Remember you're not going to win an argument, so apologising and taking the blame is likely your best bet.

"This must be difficult for you. We'll get through it together."

. . . .

"Isn't it wonderful that we have each other and that I can help out!"

. . . .

"Dad, I'm sorry you are upset. Your doctor told you that you have some memory loss. Here is your wallet."

. . . .

"Mum, I understand that you're frustrated that you can't find your favourite earrings. It's upsetting when you think you've lost a treasured possession. Let's go look for them together."

. . . .

"Dad, I know you're frustrated with me. Let me show you that your shoes are in the bedroom."

. . . .

"Mum, I know the ringing phone makes you nervous. I've asked the pharmacy to call my number instead of yours. I will take care of everything."

PREVENTION

Following are tips to consider to help prevent these actions from occurring again.

- **KEEP A JOURNAL TO DETERMINE IF THERE ARE TIMES OF DAY OR SITUATIONS THAT CAN CAUSE MUM TO BECOME PARANOID.** For example, Mum could get nervous with all the questions she's asked at the doctor's. Your journal notes will remind you that Mum likes to play cards. So take a deck along with you to the next appointment.

- **TALK WITH OTHER FAMILY MEMBERS ABOUT A SAFE PLACE TO STORE VALUABLES.** This allows for your family to all agree and know the location if they need to retrieve items to show Mum.

- **LOOK FOR WAYS TO HELP MUM MAINTAIN CONTROL OF AS MUCH IN HER LIFE AS SHE IS CAPABLE OF DOING.** If you're going to move her summer clothes to the spare room wardrobe, make sure she knows and ask her to help. That can keep her from feeling she is losing her independence.

HIDING/MISPLACING THINGS/RUMMAGING

When my husband and I moved in with my in-laws, we learned early on we couldn't leave my mother-in-law home by herself. We'd go out and when we'd return she'd have put all the rubbish in the recycling bin and vice versa. One time we got home and she'd taken all the teaspoons out of the drawer and hidden them. We looked for them everywhere.

Then three or four days later, back they were in the drawer where they belong. I never know what tomorrow will bring, but we try to find the humour in everything.

— Alinda L.

WHY DOES THIS HAPPEN?

When Mum hides things – like Alinda's family experienced – she may not realise what the items are or that they belong to someone else. She is not intentionally trying to hide an important item such as teaspoons. Because of her disease, she just doesn't understand.

Rummaging through cupboards and drawers is something Dad may do out of boredom. He may feel a sense of loss at times and may react by searching for things. His confused efforts may demonstrate his emotional losses. He also may be hoarding or hiding his things in an effort to keep his familiar possessions safe.

We know that unmet needs may contribute to these actions, so trying to understand the cause behind them will help you deal with the issue.

(Emotional • Social • Physical • Environmental)

Does the person have an unmet need that is causing the memory or behavioural symptom?

CARE APPROACHES

* If items go missing, react calmly. Mum will either have forgotten that she moved them in the first place or where she put them. If questioned, she may become upset, angry or feel that you are accusing her unfairly. Assume that she is just trying to keep these items safe and together look for the missing items.

* Help Dad maintain a regular routine. Give him things to do during the day to reinforce that routine. Perhaps ask for his assistance caring for the family dog. He could help feed and walk the dog at the same times each day.

- Lock up any valuables such as jewellery, cheque books, important papers, keys and credit cards. Install locks on cupboards and drawers, if necessary.

- Keep an eye on the post. If important post starts to disappear, consider getting a post office box or change the address to your home for important items.

- Encourage positive rummaging. Put together a purse with lots of things for Mum or a tool box with nuts and bolts for Dad. Find a pack of cards and ask Dad to organise or sort by suit or colour. Ask your spouse to sort a drawer of socks and find matched pairs.

- Observe Dad to determine if he is hiding items. The next time he can't find his hearing aid, you'll know where to look. Note this in your journal for the benefit of other family members.

- If hiding things becomes a big problem, consider installing a surveillance camera in the home.

- Regularly check the rubbish before it is put out. You will avoid the stress of an important item being thrown away. Keep rubbish bins covered and out of sight.

- Get an extra set of things such as Dad's favourite hat or Mum's TV remote control. This will make replacement faster and easier.

STARTING THE CONVERSATION

When things go missing, panic and frustration are the natural responses. Maintain your composure and try not to show your frustration or irritation. Dad could become anxious, especially if he has no memory or understanding of what's missing. It's easier to just apologise and take the blame and redirect him into a meaningful activity.

*"Dad, I'm sorry we can't find your book. I'll look for it later.
I am sure it will turn up."*

. . . .

*"Dad, I probably misplaced the remote control myself.
Don't worry, I'll find it."*

. . . .

*"Dad, it looks like you're looking for something in the drawer.
Can I help you?"*

. . . .

*"Mum, your scarf is not in this drawer. Why don't we
take a walk and look for it later."*

. . . .

*"Let's leave your glasses on your dresser Mum, where we
know we can both find them."*

. . . .

*"Mum, I know you're upset you can't find your make-up compact.
Let's go to the shop and buy a new one!"*

PREVENTION

Following are tips to consider to help prevent these actions from occurring again.

- **TO HELP PREVENT THE FRUSTRATION OF LOST ITEMS, SET ASIDE TIME TO GET ORGANISED.** Tidy cupboards, de-clutter drawers and keep only the essentials. Take time to donate unused items to charity to maintain a clutter-free environment.

- **PLAN OUT MEANINGFUL ACTIVITIES BEFORE EACH DAY TO HELP AVOID BOREDOM.** Assign Mum simple household tasks such as dusting furniture or folding clothes, taking a walk or building a memory book. A schedule and routine could help keep her engaged in the day.

- **HELP YOUR SPOUSE SUCCEED IN HIS ENVIRONMENT.** Labelling drawers and cupboards when he is resting or sleeping, for example, will provide cues and help him have successful days.

HOSTILITY

My brother was diagnosed with Alzheimer's disease on his 59th birthday, which was devastating news for our family. He occasionally became unfriendly and resistant, and blamed the world for what had happened to him. My brother had been a driving instructor and he had been used to giving instructions while in the car.

Sometimes we'd be driving and he'd reach over and pull the hand brake. One time he did that on a wet night and we went into a skid, right in front of an oncoming vehicle. I straightened up the car and then pulled over and laid into him. He threw his hands up in the air, got out of the car and started to walk. We followed slowly behind him until he'd walked off his hostility. In the future, when he would try to distract me while I was driving, I would ask someone close to him to intervene or I would pull over again and allow him the opportunity to walk.

—Joe V.

WHY DOES THIS HAPPEN?

Joe's brother became hostile or belligerent because he had lost the ability to understand or remember. Keep in mind that Joe's brother had years of experience where he helped others by intervening in their driving. He is going back to those experiences and believes he's helping someone drive. It's important for families to understand the disease is the culprit.

Let's face it, dementia changes everything, including the person with the disease. He may be pleasantly confused or become agitated and challenging. His opposition or resistance and negative attitude all are expressions of his confusion. Understanding the person's life story can help you manage these situations.

(Emotional • Social • Physical • Environmental)

Does the person have an unmet need that is causing the memory or behavioural symptom?

CARE APPROACHES

* Your demeanor and a confident and helpful tone will show in your face and voice. When Mum opposes your request, keep your body relaxed and your tone of voice even.

* When something upsets Dad, keep your emotions in check. If you insist that Dad change his shirt for example, he will resist. Step away and try approaching Dad later to change his shirt.

* Hostility is masking what Grandpa does not know. For example, he may not know the last time he washed and changed clothes. To curtail the hostility, apologise and take the blame, even if it's not your fault.

- Opposition is a sign that Dad knows he is losing control. Set the environment up for success. For instance, if you are going for a walk, have his shoes and coat ready by the door.

- Involve Dad in easy decisions about his day. This can be as simple as asking his opinion about the colour of shirt he would like to wear. Anything that can engage him in the decision-making process about his life will help.

- Routines and rituals are useful. These activities will help him feel that rhythm in life. If Dad watched "Countdown" every afternoon, make sure he still has the opportunity to do that.

- Bring up a pleasant or favourite subject like his hole-in-one on the golf course or his famous barbecues. This could completely change his mood.

- Create happy and meaningful moments. Keep Mum busy doing things she likes, such as sorting the post or arranging flowers.

- If hostility leads to an outburst, look for opportunities to lighten the mood. Changing the subject or diverting attention may calm the situation. For example, if you try to remove old newspapers and Mum becomes resistant and hostile, leave the papers and invite her to the kitchen for some tea.

STARTING THE CONVERSATION

If you've always been close to Dad, you could be an easy target for his opposition. Those with dementia often lash out in frustration at the ones they care about most. Sometimes you just need to let Dad vent his anger. Try to empathise and focus on his feelings rather than the negative actions that he's exhibiting. Often the less said, the better.

"Dad, I know you're upset with me now. When you're ready to talk, I'm here for you."

. . . .

"Mum, I'm sorry I stepped in to tie your shoes. I thought you needed help, but I should have asked."

. . . .

"Dad, I know it's hard to wait for your grandson to mow the lawn. While he's on his way, tell me about growing up in Manchester."

. . . .

"We are going to meet friends soon. Let's get you showered before we go."

. . . .

"I am sorry this is happening. I can see you are upset. Can we sit and talk about it?"

. . . .

"Mum, I know you're really good at baking chocolate cakes. But why don't I help so you can show me your secrets."

PREVENTION

Following are tips to consider to help prevent these actions from occurring again.

- **INVOLVE THE FAMILY TO LEARN ABOUT THE BEST APPROACHES TO KEEP DAD CALM.** Making a journal could help identify a particular rocking chair that soothes, a blanket, a favourite dessert or a person who has a calming effect.

- **DETERMINE MUM'S "HOT BUTTONS" TO MINIMISE HOSTILITY.** If you know Mum hates broccoli, look for other healthy vegetable options.

- **FOCUS ON SIMPLIFYING THE ENVIRONMENT TO HELP PREVENT OUTBURSTS.** If Dad "loses" sweaters, trousers etc. and his room is messy, then tidy up his space. Organise Mum's wardrobe to display fewer choices and transfer items to a basket. Label shelves and cabinets and have just essential items in the bathroom. Put an entire outfit on one hanger.

JUDGEMENT

Mum called upset one day because my father was going to buy a new car with only limited funds in the bank. When Dad came home from the dealer, he told us he was signing the papers the next day and he was paying cash.

When we tried to argue and reason that if he used all the money to buy a car, there wouldn't be any money left for him and Mum to live and eat. He said "It's my money and I'll do whatever I want with it," while my Mum just sat there and cried. We talked to Mum about appointing a power of attorney, and that was the turning point. The next day, she put a stop on their account and that was the first step in taking over their affairs.

— Stephanie R.

WHY DOES THIS HAPPEN?

Dementia often impacts not only memory, but also insight and judgment. In trying to maintain control, Stephanie's father nearly drained their bank account. Judgment problems could put Dad at risk in many areas of his life.

From the inability to select appropriate clothing for the weather to responding to a special offer in the mail, judgment problems could make Dad extremely vulnerable. It's important for family members to try to find ways to shield him and to protect the family's interests, as Stephanie's family did.

(Emotional • Social • Physical • Environmental)

Does the person have an unmet need that is causing the memory or behavioural symptom?

CARE APPROACHES

* If Dad is vulnerable to phone scams, turn the ringer off on the telephone.

* If Dad is answering the phone, learn who he's speaking with.

* Scammers target older adults because they are thought to be more trusting. When Dad is napping, register his number with the Telephone Preference Service (TPS).

* Look for unusual activity. For example, large volumes of unsolicited post addressed to Mum could mean that her personal information is at risk. Consider a P.O. Box or having post sent to your address. Check the outgoing post with her writing on it.

* Befriend Grandma's neighbours and ask if they would be willing to

help keep an eye out for suspicious activity and strangers.

- Perform daily activity checks on Dad's accounts and be prepared to cancel bank accounts or place limits on his credit cards if necessary.

- Limit the amount of cash he has at any one time.

- Be aware of Dad's purchases and keep them visible. Dad may not have been acting recklessly or extravagantly in his spending. He may have forgotten that he has purchased certain items and will repeatedly buy the same thing. Keep an eye out for receipts and return items if necessary.

- Observe Mum with visitors – new friends and even old friends. Make sure they know that Mum could be giving away items of value when she is confused. Keep trinkets or baked goods in the freezer to give to family, friends and neighbours who drop by so that Mum doesn't risk giving away valuables.

- If Mum tries to give away a valuable, it might be time to store those in a locked box.

- Sit down with Dad and discuss his charitable giving and develop a plan together. Put it on the refrigerator and help him stick with it.

- Help protect Dad's dignity and self-esteem by including him as much as possible in decisions that affect his life. Hold a monthly "meeting" with Dad to go over his bills and statements.

- Make safety a priority. Be confident in knowing that drastic measures are often necessary to protect the person. For example, if Dad still wants to drive the car but can't remember where the shop is, you may need to take away the keys. If he still insists, telling him the car has broken down may help.

STARTING THE CONVERSATION

Poor judgment might be one of the first things you notice in your family member with dementia. This difficult action could lead to role reversal, where you are now the protector, ensuring that Dad is safe. During this transition time, it's important to be helpful and positive while reassuring Dad through important decisions that impact his life.

"You've always done a great job with your bills, Dad.
Let's work together and get things organised."

. . . .

"Dad, the bank wants us to be very careful with our accounts
and keep everything private, OK?"

. . . .

"You know, Mum, there are greedy people out there. I won't
let them take advantage of you so I put your name on the
Telephone Preference Service register."

. . . .

"May I please help you with your cheque book?"

. . . .

"Thank you for allowing me to play a role in your care."

. . . .

"Things in the world have changed so much, Dad. I understand your
frustration. Let me take care of paying your council tax."

PREVENTION

Following are tips to consider to help prevent these actions from occurring again.

- **TAKE TIME TO ASSESS THE HOME FOR SAFETY ISSUES.** Sharp objects in the kitchen (like knives), medications that are unsecured and chemicals under the sink or in the garage could be dangerous for someone with poor judgement.

- **TAKE PROACTIVE STEPS TO WORK WITH MUM'S LEGAL AND FINANCIAL ADVISORS.** Arrange Power of Attorney, preferably appointing a close family member.

MEDICATION MISMANAGEMENT

When visiting Mum we would find medication that hadn't been taken for as much as a week at a time. We also had growing concern that Mum's "off" days were because she had taken a few days' tablets at once.

She wasn't eating properly and lost at least three stone; even her dog suffered from a lack of food and exercise. We were at our wit's end. Both my brother and I live a distance away from Mum and couldn't be there every day. I dreaded the phone ringing and just didn't know which way to turn for help.

— Caroline W.

WHY DOES THIS HAPPEN?

Ageing adults often take multiple medications. Add to that the confusion that dementia may cause, as Caroline's family discovered, and you have a recipe for disaster.

Mismanaging medications can lead to side effects such as drowsiness, irritability and insomnia. Accompanied with dementia, this situation could diminish a person's quality of life.

More than anything, you need to help your family member make sure she is taking her medications correctly. This will help prevent medication mishaps and adverse drug reactions.

(Emotional • Social • Physical • Environmental)

Does the person have an unmet need that is causing the memory or behavioural symptom?

CARE APPROACHES

* If Mum can no longer be an advocate for herself, you will need to be her eyes and ears. Work with her doctor, and learn the drug's purpose and possible side effects.

* Try sending questions to her doctor prior to an appointment to ensure all your questions are answered.

* Maintain open communication with your spouse's pharmacist. This will help to reduce the risk of medication interactions.

* If a family member is having difficulty swallowing, ask the pharmacist if the medicine is available as a liquid or if you can crush it and add to a pudding or yoghurt that he likes.

- If Dad takes medications multiple times during the day, you may need to call and remind him or leave notes.

- Observe your family member for any potential side effects. She may be unable to understand, recognise, make the connection or describe the changes she feels.

- Mum may become confused when taking multiple pills. She could try to spit them out. Stay with her and make sure she swallows the pills. Check sinks, toilets and dustbins as well.

STARTING THE CONVERSATION

Medication management is an important part of Mum's quality of life. Dementia could cause Mum to confuse prescriptions and forget to take medications. Clear communication can help make sure she's safe. Start with a positive facial expression, use clear words and avoid over-explaining. Point to the medication and demonstrate how to take the pills all while giving step-by-step directions.

"I'm going to help you with your pills. Let's start with the first one."

. . . .

Say, "Here is your pill," rather than "Your pills are on the table ."

. . . .

"Here's the white pill. Place it in your hand. Put it on your tongue. Take a drink of water."

. . . .

"This pill helps your heart, Mum."

. . . .

"You need to take these pills, Dad, to keep you feeling good."

PREVENTION

Following are tips to consider to help prevent these actions from occurring again.

- **STORE MEDICINES SAFELY.** A pill organiser can help. Find them at any pharmacy.

- **REVIEW THE LIST OF MEDICATIONS WITH YOUR DOCTOR AND PHARMACIST REGULARLY.** Does Mum need to take every pill? Reducing unnecessary medications can simplify your care giving experience.

- **KEEP A MEDICATION TRACKER.** Record times, doses, the doctor who ordered the medication and any side effects or symptoms of each prescription Mum is taking. Note if she should avoid certain foods or take medicines on an empty stomach. Be sure to include over-the-counter medicines. Keep a list on your computer and a hard copy in a safe place at home. Carry a list in your purse or wallet.

- **READ ABOUT MEDICATIONS.** Ask for literature about each medication that your family member is taking and refer to it as needed for any questions.

MOOD CHANGES

My mother-in-law, who has dementia, lived with me, my husband and two small children for two years. She could be in the best mood – calm and happy – until we tried to help her get dressed or give her medications. "I don't need your help," she would say. "I've been doing this all my life."

If we attempted to encourage her to change outfits after wearing the same one for two days, her mood would change suddenly when she realised she was forgetting. If we could distract her by sitting outside on a nice day or inviting her to watch her favourite TV show, her happy mood would quickly return.

—Julie D.

WHY DOES THIS HAPPEN?

Throughout the progression of dementia, mood changes may occur and sometimes can be a complete surprise, as Julie observed with her mother-in-law. Your family member may experience difficult mental, emotional and even physical challenges that cause these increasing mood changes.

When a person can't remember or is constantly confused she may be frustrated, fearful and even fight the changes. It's no wonder that mood swings are a common problem among those who have dementia.

It is wise to accept and anticipate that dementia is the cause of the mood changes. Avoid thinking that she is having personality changes. Separate her, the person you know and care about, from the disease and its symptoms.

(Emotional • Social • Physical • Environmental)

Does the person have an unmet need that is causing the memory or behavioural symptom?

CARE APPROACHES

* Maintain and establish new routines if necessary. By filling Mum's day with set activities, she won't be so prone to mood changes. When Mum understands that after breakfast she always reads the paper and gets dressed for the day, she knows what's coming next.

* If you tell Mum to get dressed she may become overwhelmed by the multiple steps involved in the task. Break it into simple steps, such as taking Mum to the wardrobe and deciding on an outfit for the day.

* Asking Dad what he wants for dinner requires a lot of thinking. Why not give him a choice between roast chicken or casserole?

- Simplifying his living space will help. Avoid clutter, label his wardrobe shelves, reduce items in cupboards and on his work surfaces.

- Keeping her physical environment constant and calm will help minimise mood swings. Turn down the TV volume if it's distracting. Keep redecorating to a minimum.

- If Grandma's in a bad mood, ask her to help with simple tasks around the house. By dusting, polishing shoes, sorting socks or folding laundry, she will likely feel useful.

- If a mood change occurs, redirect Dad to a meaningful activity, such as walking the family dog around the block.

- Avoid stress as much as possible. If you think Mum would get nervous about an upcoming family reunion, tell her about it just a few days beforehand and keep details to a minimum.

- If Dad is upset about missing his favourite TV show, apologise and give a reason, like dinner was started a little late. This may lighten his mood.

- Pay Mum a compliment or offer praise to make her smile and improve her mood.

- Sometimes laughter is the best medicine. Look for ways to inject humour into Dad's day, like watching old episodes of "Dad's Army."

STARTING THE CONVERSATION

Mood changes can impact anyone involved in Mum's care. By controlling your own emotions, you can help prevent mood changes from ruining everyone's day and may even improve your family member's mood. When Mum is in a bad mood, try to limit her choices and keep the conversation simple.

"I'm excited about the family reunion tomorrow, Mum," instead of "The family reunion starts tomorrow, Mum, we need to pick out your dress, do your nails and get your hair done."

. . . .

"Would you like porridge or toast today for breakfast?"

. . . .

"Mum, I'm sorry I rushed you during your shower. Next time we'll start earlier."

. . . .

"I know you hate to go to the optician, but let's get a cup of tea afterwards."

. . . .

"Gosh, Dad, I can't find pairs for these socks. You've always been good at this. Would you help me sort them, please?"

. . . .

"Dad, I know you're down today and really missing Mum. I miss her too. Let's go and look at the photo album."

PREVENTION

Following are tips to consider to help prevent these actions from occurring again.

- **BE MINDFUL OF DAD'S SCHEDULE AND ADAPT IF NECESSARY.** For example, the whole process of bathing and dressing involves a certain level of energy to accomplish these once-routine tasks. Schedule them during the time of day when he is most calm, hydrated, free of hunger pangs and has some energy.

- **MOODS CAN BE DIFFICULT TO PREDICT, SO KEEP A JOURNAL OF WHAT'S CAUSING THESE CHANGES AND THEIR TRIGGERS.** Understand that your family member's abilities can change on a daily basis, so be prepared to assist.

- **TALK TO THE DOCTOR ABOUT YOUR SPOUSE'S MOOD CHANGES.** It will be important for your doctor to understand if she is losing weight, crying or sleeping too much, which could be signs of depression.

REPETITION

I was about 10 years old when I realised something was happening to my great-grandmother that I couldn't explain. When I was at their house, it seemed like Mimi was always going back to the places she had just cleaned and cleaning them again.

She compulsively applied her makeup and nail polish all day until her face and nails were caked half an inch thick.

My great-grandpa would go around behind her and "fix things." Whenever our family was together, we just went along with this repetitive behaviour.

— Kelly R.

WHY DOES THIS HAPPEN?

Because of Mum's memory loss, she could repeat the same phrase, question or task over and over again. While this behaviour is not likely dangerous, it can be frustrating for you and other family members. Or puzzling for children, as Kelly discovered.

You might notice that Dad is going through the same actions from his prior work or interests, for example. This could indicate that Dad might be missing some structure in his life. Or this action could represent boredom. Discovering the causes of Dad's behaviour could help cut down on the repetitive actions.

(Emotional • Social • Physical • Environmental)

Does the person have an unmet need that is causing the memory or behavioural symptom?

CARE APPROACHES

* Encourage Grandma to find the answer to the question she keeps repeating. For example, if she keeps asking the time, make sure a clock is visible to her. A digital clock is easier for people with dementia to understand.

* Dad may become anxious about future events such as an outing, which can lead to repeated questioning. When Dad has an upcoming appointment or event to attend, he may keep asking, "When do we leave?" Avoid mentioning the trip until a short time before it takes place.

* If Dad is continually asking to go home even if he is living with close family, reassure him that he is safe and loved. Find something in his environment that reminds him of home, or look at a photo album.

- Try letting the repetitive actions run their course without trying to "hush" him. Repetition is thought to be a comfort measure similar to physically rocking back and forth.

- Ask Grandma to tell you more about her concerns. Sometimes just drawing out the conversation can stop the repetition.

- If Mum is using repetitive phrases or movements, this can be due to noisy or stressful surroundings, or boredom. Redirect her to the kitchen for a snack, for example.

- Keep Dad engaged in meaningful activities he once enjoyed. Perhaps there was a hobby such as painting that he loved that you could redirect him to.

- If Mum is constantly drumming her nails on the table, give her something to occupy her hands such as a ball of wool.

- Try distracting Mum with her favourite treat or playing her favourite song when she is repeating words or questions.

- If Mum becomes fixated on an object in the room, distract her and remove it. If it's something that cannot be moved, lead Mum into the bedroom to fold clothes.

STARTING THE CONVERSATION

Repetitive actions can really test a family carer's patience. However, Mum can't help that she can't remember. Successful communication could help ease Mum's worries and frustrations. Listen for clues to understanding Mum's actions then try redirecting her to a different topic. Your tone of voice and body language will help set the stage for a great day.

"Mum, you keep getting your shoes out of the cupboard then putting them away. Are you anxious about the doctor's appointment today?"

"Mum, you keep asking me what's for dinner and it is still several hours away. Why don't we have an apple?"

"I'm sorry if I seem frustrated today, Mum. I am just having a bad day. Let's make some tea."

"Dad, you keep pacing by the door. I know you're nervous about what time your sister is coming. She'll be here soon!"

"Dad, 'Deal or No Deal' is on in a few hours. In the meantime, let's do the word search from the paper today."

PREVENTION

Following are tips to consider to help prevent these actions from occurring again.

- **TUNE IN TO DAD'S DAILY ROUTINES.** For example, be consistent with walks, pet care and TV shows.

- **IDENTIFY AND STEER DAD TOWARD A FEW OF HIS KEY DISTRACTIONS THAT COULD HELP TO CHANGE HIS COURSE.** Find a CD with his favourite song, locate his favourite book in the bookcase and set out a photo of his prize-winning fisherman's catch.

- **SURROUNDING HIM WITH LOVE AND ATTENTION CAN HELP EASE REPETITIVE ACTIONS.** Have family and friends around to support him and visit.

- **KEEP YOUR JOURNAL CURRENT WITH CLUES THAT COULD LEAD TO DAD'S REPETITIVE ACTIONS.** Understanding those triggers can help you prevent the repetition.

SEXUALLY INAPPROPRIATE BEHAVIOUR

Dad wanted to invite his brother, who has dementia, over for lunch. So I volunteered to help prepare the meal. When I greeted my uncle, we hugged. But to my surprise, the hug lingered while he ran his hands down my back.

I didn't know how to react so I changed the subject. Then, as I was bringing lunch to the table, my uncle commented about my pretty legs. After the second incident, I realised this was not the action of my uncle, but the disease. I went back to the kitchen and took a few deep breaths. As the day went on, I was prepared to distract my uncle if anything happened again.

— Anonymous

WHY DOES THIS HAPPEN?

Dementia can reduce a person's inhibitions, which may expose his private thoughts, feelings and behaviours of a personal nature, including sex. That's what this family was observing. These actions are symptoms of the disease and sometimes the person is just looking for a human connection.

He may use language that people have never heard him use before and which seems very out of character. Or, he may have impaired impulse control. For example, your family member, who may have always been reserved, could begin to remove his clothes in public. Such behaviours are not only embarrassing to watch, they could jeopardise the person's dignity and safety. Understanding that this is the disease talking and not the person will help you cope.

(Emotional • Social • Physical • Environmental)

Does the person have an unmet need that is causing the memory or behavioural symptom?

CARE APPROACHES

* With this being a sensitive situation, try not to panic. The more upset you become, the more upset Dad will become. Remain calm with relaxed body language.

* If Dad comes down for breakfast without his trousers, it may not be a sexual gesture. He may just have forgotten how to get dressed. Direct him to the bedroom and help him get dressed.

* Stand near the bathroom with Grandma's clothing when she is getting dressed. Be ready to cover her if she comes out undressed.

- Make sure clothing is easy to get on and off. Consider Velcro rather than buttons.

- If Dad is making an inappropriate comment to a waitress, redirect him by telling him the specials for the day or asking what he wants to drink.

- Look for new things to do together. Teach Dad a new board game or song to redirect if he is acting inappropriately.

- Some people with dementia crave textures like soft fleece or cotton. If Dad becomes fidgety try having him hold a pillow, a stuffed animal, a blanket or even a squeeze stress ball.

- Give Mum more attention. She needs to know you are there as she goes through this sometimes frightening journey.

- Sitting or kneeling with Dad on the same level may reduce his fidgeting. Then try holding his hand or offering him something else to hold.

STARTING THE CONVERSATION

Inappropriate behaviour can fluster a family carer and may put you on edge, anticipating that it could happen at any time. Knowing the disease is causing the action and not the person, your best strategy is to preserve his dignity. A confident and understanding attitude will help you divert the situation without embarrassing your family member.

"Dad, instead of fidgeting with your zip, do you have to go to the bathroom? If not, can you help me fold these tea towels?"

. . . .

"Dad, don't touch Mum while she's trying to nap. Let's go into the living room and turn on the TV. What would you like to watch?"

. . . .

"Dad, are you too warm? Is that why you're taking off your shirt?" "Let's leave your shirt on since it's cold," rather than, "Don't take off your shirt!"

. . . .

"Dad, she is really pretty, but she is very busy answering the phone. Let's go sit down and read a magazine while waiting for the doctor."

PREVENTION

Following are tips to consider to help prevent these actions from occurring again.

- **REASSURE YOUR SPOUSE REGULARLY.** He may be experiencing a need to be touched by another human. The disease is causing him to express it in the only way he knows how. Hold his hand, massage his shoulders or give him a hug.

- **BE AWARE OF DAD'S CLOTHING CHOICES.** If he is too hot, his underwear too tight or the material of his shirt scratching his skin, he may try to undress.

- **PRACTICE AND ROLE-PLAY THE CONVERSATION.** Because this is such a sensitive subject, you'll want to be prepared to avoid embarrassment and preserve their self-esteem. Choose your words and practice how you will redirect. Role-play with another family member so you are confident and prepared in the future.

SOCIAL WITHDRAWAL

Dad would get into silent moods, not looking at or talking to Mum for the entire day. He still had days when he was lucid and responsive, so the silent days caused Mum to worry that he was slipping away entirely. One evening, when I stopped at my parents' house, Mum warned me that it had been "one of those days," so I told Mum to get out of the house to clear her head.

There was sport on the telly, so if Dad wanted to watch the game and not talk, that was fine with me. An hour or so of complete silence had passed before he turned to me and said, "Where are my wine gums?" They are his all-time favourite sweets. When Mum came home, I assured her that he was still in there and we laughed about the only five words he spoke all day.

It occurred to me on my way home that if Dad were to die overnight, his last spoken words would be "wine gums." I circled back to my parents' house and awakened my sleeping Dad to tell him I loved him. I asked him if he loved me too so that those words would be his last words if he were to die suddenly.

— Dan W.

WHY DOES THIS HAPPEN?

Socialisation has many benefits. But for the person with dementia, it often feels safer just to stay home. They could be nervous about forgetting a name or failing to recognise an important person in their life.

Social withdrawal also can be caused by a desire to avoid embarrassment and having his friends see him struggling. Most people know that dementia is not "going away," so depression may set in, which might be what Dan's family was seeing with their father.

By being patient and finding simple, joyful moments, Dan and his family were still able to connect with their loved one.

(Emotional • Social • Physical • Environmental)

Does the person have an unmet need that is causing the memory or behavioural symptom?

CARE APPROACHES

* Dementia could be difficult for Dad's friends. Surround him with friends who best understand and can support him. Help organise a barbeque in the garden for those kinds of supportive friends.

* Reassure your family member that you will go with him for lunch with his friends to offer support if needed.

* One of the benefits of socialising is having a good laugh. If Dad is apprehensive about going out with friends, put on a favourite film that always makes him smile and laugh.

- Every home has a social hub, whether it's the kitchen, the living room or the garden. Make sure your spouse is always present and included in conversations and family activities.

- Plan outings with extended family and friends. He may be reluctant to go to the family reunion, so ask his brother or another trusted relative to attend with him. Or plan smaller outings with relatives.

- During a large family get-together, remind family members that it would be best to try to talk with him one-on-one in a quiet room so as not to overwhelm him.

- Plan appropriate activities that won't make Mum anxious. When the grandchildren are round, instead of playing board games, ask her to hold the garden hose while they are watering flowers.

- Try asking Mum to be social in different ways. If she says "no" when you try to schedule a lunch, suggest that you invite one friend over to the house instead. If that doesn't work, suggest you call her friend on the phone later that afternoon.

- To encourage social activities, use Mum's life story to uncover meaningful outings. If she always got her hair done, schedule this activity and invite her good friend along too.

- Work on building meaningful memories together. If she doesn't already have a scrapbook, go looking for pictures that represent various stages in her life. Ask about the people and places that were important to her.

STARTING THE CONVERSATION

Isolation may only worsen dementia and lead to depression. As a carer, you almost need to be a social secretary for your family member, always encouraging her to stay socially active. Remember what Mum has always liked to do and talk openly with her about continuing those interests.

"I'd be so happy if you would come with me to church,"
rather than, "Would you like to go to church?"

. . . .

"Mum, I know you didn't want to go to lunch with Shirley.
But Shirley wants to see you because she has some important news.
Let's get your coat."

. . . .

"If you don't want to go to coffee with the lads today, let's
walk around the block and see your old friend Joe."

. . . .

"Mum, I know you're nervous about going to bridge club.
Let me go with you and be your coach."

. . . .

"Dad, why don't you come into the kitchen and join in the
conversation. Tell us one of your famous fishing stories."

. . . .

"Mum, should we go out to lunch with your sister or have
her round to our house?"

PREVENTION

Following are tips to consider to help prevent these actions from occurring again.

● **SET UP A MONTHLY SOCIAL SCHEDULE FOR YOUR FAMILY MEMBER.** Encourage Mum's friends, relatives and neighbours to get together once a month for a visit. Keep it on the same day each month. Keep a calendar in Mum's view to see all her upcoming social commitments.

● **OBSERVE GRANDAD'S REACTION TO DIFFERENT PEOPLE.** Does his face light up when he sees a certain friend or family member? Consider recording thoughts and feelings about what you have learned and what you know works for your family member.

● **UNDERSTAND THE PERSON'S LIFE STORY.** Did he go to lunch with friends? Did she talk on the phone with family? Did he like to entertain the grandchildren? By maintaining his regular social activities, Dad will still feel connected.

WANDERING

When my husband started wandering, he would always go to the fire station down the road. When I realised this, I went to the station with a picture of him and I gave them my name, address and phone number.

The firemen would take him to the break room and get him a cup of coffee while they called me. One Sunday morning, I discovered he was gone and the firemen hadn't seen him. Turns out he'd gone to church, and in his pyjamas.

Then there was that one time when he tried to go out in my blouse and my cropped trousers. I laughed so hard and he was so proud he could still make me laugh.

— Evelyn H.

WHY DOES THIS HAPPEN?

Many people with dementia pace or roam, perhaps out of nervous energy or because they are looking for things to do. Your spouse also may be trying to fulfill a physical need such as thirst, hunger, using the bathroom or exercise. This behaviour can become more serious, however, if a person with dementia tries to leave the house, like Evelyn's husband.

Once you identify what he is trying to achieve, you can start to find ways to deal with the underlying issue. This could reduce your frustration and worry, and help him retain his independence.

(Emotional • Social • Physical • Environmental)

Does the person have an unmet need that is causing the memory or behavioural symptom?

CARE APPROACHES

* Make a path in the home where it is safe and comfortable for Mum to wander or pace. Closing off certain parts of a room or locking doors can help you achieve this goal. Such paths can also be created outdoors – in a garden, for example.

* Simplify the environment. Relocate decorative furniture such as the small antique table. Use only a few larger pieces of furniture that are solid in colour.

* Remove items that could be difficult to see, such as glass figurines, small picture frames and vases. De-cluttering the main living spaces can help Dad move about freely.

- Install barriers and fences in the garden to help ensure that Mum doesn't wander into unsafe territory or away from home. Place large flowerpots near a small opening.

- Create inviting areas. For example, Grandma's garden could have a bench, bird feeders and garden ornaments. When she is enjoying herself, this may stop her from wandering further.

- If Dad is determined to leave, try not to confront him, as this could be upsetting. Try to get him to put on appropriate clothing. Accompany him and then divert his attention so that you can both return.

- If Mum is trying to leave, redirect her into a household activity, such as folding towels, or a past hobby she may have enjoyed, such as gardening.

- Set aside 20 minutes a day for regular exercise to minimise restlessness. A supervised walk around the park will help relieve her agitation, anxiety and boredom.

- If Dad is wandering, try to get out for a car ride. A change in scenery and fresh air may help.

- When taking Dad on an outing, try to pick places that are less crowded; for example, the local coffee shop rather than a large supermarket.

STARTING THE CONVERSATION

Although wandering is frightening, there's usually an underlying cause that communication could help you work out and stop. Approaching the situation cautiously, being ready with a diversion and reassuring the family member will make this behaviour less scary for everyone.

"Dad, can I join you on that walk?" or "Where are you going?"

. . . .

"Mum, I know you're anxious to get to the shop. Let's sit down and make a list first."

. . . .

"Mum, I notice that you keep walking to the window and looking out at the garden. Let's go buy a few pansies, your favourite flower, and you can help me plant them."

. . . .

"Dad, I notice that you keep pacing between your bedroom and the coat stand. It's OK. I'll remind you when it's time to meet your friends and go with you."

. . . .

"Mum, I see you're in the neighbour's garden. Aren't her flowers beautiful? Come back to your house and I will get us something to drink."

. . . .

"I'm sorry we didn't get out for our walk today since it was raining. I waited too long. Why don't we go for a drive instead?"

PREVENTION

Following are tips to consider to help prevent these actions from occurring again.

- **BE PREPARED IF YOUR LOVED ONE WANDERS OR BECOMES LOST.** Make sure Dad has a piece of identification always on him or consider an ID bracelet. You may sew identification into his jacket near the collar so that it is not easily removed. Always have a current photo available if you need to report him lost or missing.

- **EDUCATE OTHERS.** Tell local shop owners and trusted neighbours about his disease and give them your contact details and a current photo.

- **MAKE YOUR HOME SAFE.** Position locks high or low on the door, in an unfamiliar location. A "stop" sign or "do not enter" sign on exit doors and stairwells may help.

- **KEEP A JOURNAL FOR A COUPLE OF WEEKS TO HELP IDENTIFY – AND REMOVE – ANY TRIGGERS.** Try to find out if his walking has a purpose; don't presume that he is wandering. He may be trying to get to work, for example.

- **ENSURE CONSTANT SUPERVISION.** People who wander need constant supervision to be safe. This is not something you should try to do alone for extended periods of time. Accept help.

Help for the Carer

It's likely you have discovered that one of the challenging aspects of caring for someone with dementia is managing the many emotions that often come with caring. It's important to discuss the common emotions people experience and why they happen. The following practical suggestions may help not only to manage the emotions, but also to prevent future problems. Besides, feeling less stressed and happier often leads to being a more patient carer. So everyone wins!

COMMON EMOTIONS THAT CARERS EXPERIENCE

Family carers report experiencing many emotions when caring for someone with dementia. Take a look at the list of emotions below and see how many you have felt in the last day, week, or perhaps month.

• AGITATION	• FRUSTRATION	• REACTIVE
• ANGER	• GRIEF	• RELAXED
• ANXIETY	• GUILT	• RELIEF
• COMPASSION	• HAPPINESS	• RESENTMENT
• DEPRESSION	• HELPLESSNESS	• SADNESS
• EMBARRASSMENT	• IMPATIENCE	
• FEAR	• LOVE	

As you look at the list, you may find you are experiencing several sometimes conflicting emotions at the same time; for example, love and frustration. And you may be feeling a certain emotion a little bit or very intensely. If you are angry and don't deal with that emotion, it may grow to be rage. That's one of the reasons it is important to take the time to identify your emotions.

Take a moment to note down the emotions you are feeling right now.

Many people think emotions are either "good" or "bad." The truth is emotions just are; it is what we DO with our emotions, how we handle them, that has either a positive or negative impact on our lives and on the lives of people we love. The first step in better emotion management is to identify what we are feeling.

THE CAUSES

Many factors can affect our emotional state. Think about what could be contributing to your feelings. Begin by reading the list below and ask yourself if any of these may be impacting how you are feeling now. For example, are you completely exhausted? If so, and you are feeling stressed or anxious, it is very likely that this is contributing to your feelings. As you are trying to understand the causes of your emotions, maintain an attitude of curiosity rather than judgment. For example, "I wonder what might be contributing to me feeling angry today," is more helpful than scolding yourself for feeling angry!

Below are some examples of things that could be influencing your emotions.

- Your siblings or other family members are not supporting you or pulling their fair weight.

- You have no family nearby to offer support and help with caring for your parent.

- The family is at odds on how best to support and care for Mum or Dad at home. Or your support team (family) has been distant most of your life.

- Your relationship with Mum or Dad has been strained over the years, but now they need your help.

- Because of the dementia, your relationship with Mum or Dad has changed, and there is tension because of the change in roles.

- If you are caring for a spouse who has the tendency to wander, worrying if they will leave in the middle of the night is causing you many sleepless nights, leading to exhaustion.

- You are working full time and managing your own household and family.

- You are overwhelmed with responsibility and Mum's dementia diagnosis leaves you feeling hopeless and depressed.

- You have a chronic condition, such as osteoporosis, that causes you to have pain most days.

- With all the other responsibilities in your life, exercise and nutrition have fallen off the priority list.

> *Take some time to note down what may be affecting your emotions.*

After you have discovered a few of the causes, next consider these three questions:

- Why do I have no control over this situation?

- What can I control about the situation?

- What can I influence or impact?

As you answer each of these three questions, you may find that the only control you have is how you think and react to the situation. You also may realise that you can influence the situation. For example, Dad may be frustrated because you have to help him get dressed in the morning. It's hard to change Dad's emotion, but if you took a few proactive steps to set Dad up for success, such as putting trousers and a matching shirt on the same hanger or laying his clothes out in order of how they go on, you can then just assist from a distance if needed. So, Dad feels a sense of independence, and lessens his frustration.

After doing this exercise, you can start to train your brain to spend time focusing only on what you can impact and let the worry go.

MANAGING EMOTIONS

Now that you have identified your emotions and some of the causes, here are some additional tips on managing those emotions.

- **KEEP A JOURNAL TO IDENTIFY WHAT YOU ARE FEELING.** Before you can better manage your emotions, you need to know what you are feeling. Sometimes we get so busy in our lives that we don't tune into our own emotional signals. By writing down what is going on and what you are feeling, it can help you tap into your emotions.

- **TALK WITH A FRIEND.** Sometimes talking with someone who knows and loves us can help us work out what we are feeling.

- **FIND A SUPPORT GROUP.** Look to your local faith community or Alzheimer's support group. You may find people who are also caring for someone with dementia. They can offer emotional support and additional tips for care.

- **GET HELP!** If there is a specific task that is difficult, consider asking someone else to do it. For example, if bath time becomes a struggle every time, you may find that Mum will be more cooperative with someone other than you assisting her.

- **DON'T BE AFRAID TO ASK.** How many times do you hear from your family or friends, "What can I do to help?" Well, consider taking them up on the offer or asking for help. And be creative as to where you ask for the help. What if you got a friend to organise a team of people to bring round dinner once a week? Or is there a friend who could help with lifts?

- **TAKE A BREAK.** Respite care, or a break, is not just a "nice" thing, it is a necessity when caring for someone with dementia. You wouldn't expect your mobile phone to work without recharging it, so why would you think you are able to provide endless caregiving without a break? You need to recharge, too! However, not every break has to be a week-long holiday.

- **BEGIN WITH A SHORT BREAK!** Start by writing down a list of things you enjoy doing. The list might include reading, watching TV, having coffee with a friend, talking with a friend on the phone, exercising, taking a walk, listening to music, sitting outside, cooking, crossword puzzles or any number of other things. Then, take one or two 15-minute mini-breaks each day to do something on your list. The goal is to build up the number and length of the breaks over time.

- **BE INTENTIONAL WITH YOUR BREAKS.** When you are a carer, planning ahead is important. Plan out your breaks, too. Pause and think about all the areas in your life. We all have basic needs, which include physical, emotional, creative, social, mental or intellectual and spiritual. So each day, try to make sure you are balanced and taking breaks that will fill those needs. For example, when Dad is napping, do 15 minutes of yoga. Or when Dad is watching his favourite show, read your book. Invite a friend over for lunch one day with you and Dad. When you are feeling balanced and meeting your needs, you will likely come back refreshed and better able to deal with the emotions that usually accompany caring.

- **TAKE CARE OF YOURSELF.** We all know that we should probably be taking better care of ourselves. Most of us know that getting enough sleep, attending to our medical care, eating well, exercising, having enough social support and doing things that help us enjoy life are key to good "self" care. Good self care contributes to our emotional well-being and helps us better manage stress and the other emotions that accompany caregiving.

- **ATTITUDE IS EVERYTHING.** The one thing all of us can do to feel better emotionally is to be aware of how we think about a situation. For example, do you believe that you have to do it all alone as a carer? Many carers have that belief and it makes them feel like a failure when they can't manage everything alone! Changing your attitude to, "Mum needs the best care," instead of "I must provide all the care," might mean that several people – including professionals – are involved in the care team.

- **LET IT GO.** Ask yourself if something is worth the battle – if it really matters? Often when you step back and look at a situation, what seems very important in the short term won't matter in the long run. For example, if your father is wearing clothes that don't match, it isn't harming him and, since he is at home, it really doesn't matter. By asking yourself this question, it will likely prevent you from getting upset about things you can just let go.

- **USE THIS BOOK AS A RESOURCE.** It is full of practical solutions. For example, if you find you are increasingly frustrated because your father will only wear the same shirt every day, consider buying several shirts exactly like the one he wants to wear. In this way, he will be happy that he can wear the same shirt, and you will no longer be frustrated by the situation.

Look to the following section for other resources to help you in your caring journey.

Resources

ORGANISATIONS

AGE UK
1-6 Tavistock Square
London WC1H 9NA
www.ageuk.org.uk
Advice Line: 0800 169 6565

AGE CYMRU
Tŷ John Pathy
13/14 Neptune Court
Vanguard Way
Cardiff CF24 5PJ
www.ageuk.org.uk/cymru
Tel: 029 2043 1555
Advice line: 08000 223 444

AGE NI
3 Lower Crescent
Belfast
Northern Ireland BT7 1NR
www.ageuk.org.uk/northern-ireland
Advice Line: 0808 8087575

AGE SCOTLAND
Causewayside House
160 Causewayside
Edinburgh EH9 1PR
www.ageuk.org.uk/scotland
Tel: 0845 125 9732
Helpline: 0845 125 9732

ALZHEIMER'S DISEASE INTERNATIONAL
64 Great Suffolk Street
London SE1 0BL
info@alz.co.uk
www.alz.co.uk
Tel: +44 20 79810880

ALZHEIMER'S RESEARCH UK
3 Riverside, Granta Park
Cambridge, CH21 6AD
www.alzheimersresearchuk.org
Tel: 0300 111 5555

ALZHEIMER'S SOCIETY
Devon House, 58 St Katharines Way
London E1W 1LB
www.alzheimers.org.uk
Tel: 020 7423 3500
Helpline: 0300 222 1122

ALZHEIMER'S SOCIETY – Welsh office
16 Columbus Walk
Atlantic Wharf
Cardiff CF10 4BY
www.alzheimers.org.uk
Tel: 02920 480593

ALZHEIMER'S SCOTLAND
22 Drumsheugh Gardens
Edinburgh EH3 7RN
www.alzscot.org
Tel: 0131 243 1453
Helpline: 0808 808 3000

CARERS TRUST ENGLAND
Unit 14, Bourne Court, Southend Road
Woodford Green, Essex, IG8 8HD
www.carers.org
Tel: 0844 800 4361

CARERS TRUST WALES
Third Floor, 33-35 Cathedral Road
Cardiff, CF11 9HB
www.carers.org
Tel: 0292 009 0087

THE PRINCESS ROYAL TRUST FOR CARERS (Scottish Carer's Trust)
Skypark 3, Suite 1/2, 14/18 Elliott Place
Glasgow, G3 8EP
www.carers.org
Tel: 0300 123 2008

CARERS UK
20 Great Dover Street
London
SE1 4LX
www.carersuk.org
Tel: 020 7378 4999
Advice Line: 0808 808 7777

CARERS NI
58 Howard Street
Belfast BT1 6JP
www.carersuk.org/northernireland
Advice Line: 02890 439843

CARERS SCOTLAND
The Cottage
21 Pearce Street
Glasgow GS1 3UT
www.carersuk.org/scotland
Tel: 0141 445 3070
Advice Line: 0808 808 7777

CARERS WALES
River House
Ynys Bridge Court
Cardiff CF15 9SS
www.carersuk.org/wales
Tel: 0290 811370
Advice Line: 0808 808 777

DEMENTIA ACTION ALLIANCE
www.dementiaaction.org.uk

DEMENTIA UK (Formerly "For Dementia")
6 Camden High Street
London NW1 0JH
www.dementiauk.org
Tel: 020 7874 7200

HOME INSTEAD SENIOR CARE UK
Walnut Tree Business Centre, Walnut Tree Farm
Warrington WA4 4PG
www.homeinstead.co.uk
Tel: 01925 730273

LEWY BODY SOCIETY
8 Albany Street, Edinburgh
www.lewybody.org
Tel: 0131 473 2385

NATIONAL COUNCIL FOR PALLIATIVE CARE
188 – 194 York Way
London N7 9AS
www.npc.org.uk
Tel: 020 7697 1520

SOLICITORS FOR THE ELDERLY
Suite 17, Conbar House
Mead Lane, Hertford, Hants, SG13 7AP
www.solicitorsfortheelderly.com
Tel: 0844 800 9710

THE DEMENTIA CHALLENGE
www.dementiachallenge.dh.gov.uk

PUBLICATIONS

"About Dementia", Dementia UK; http://www.dementiauk.org/information-support/about-dementia/#6

A Dignified Life, Revised and Expanded: The Best Friend's Approach to Alzheimer's Care, A Guide for Family Care Partners, by Virginia Bell, M.S.W and David Troxel, M.P.H.; www.amazon.co.uk/Dignified-Life-Revised-Expanded-Alzheimers/dp/0757316654/ref=sr_1_1?ie=UTF8&qid=1376923634&sr=8-1&keywords=a+dignified+life

Activities of Daily Living – an ADL guide for Alzheimer's Care, by Kathy Laurenhue, M.A.; (Kindle Edition) www.amazon.co.uk/Activities-Daily-Living-Alzheimers-ebook/dp/B004PGO34O/ref=sr_1_1?ie=UTF8&qid=1376923916&sr=8-1&keywords=activities+of+daily+living+-+an+ADL+guide

Alzheimer's Basic Caregiving – an ABC Guide, by Kathy Laurenhue, M.A.; (Kindle Edition) www.amazon.co.uk/Alzheimers-Basic-Caregiving-Guide-ebook/dp/B004PGNGCY/ref=sr_1_1?ie=UTF8&qid=1376924077&sr=8-1&keywords=alzheimer%27s+basic+caregiving

"Alzheimer's Disease Fact Sheet," National Institute on Aging (USA); www.nia.nih.gov/alzheimers/publication/alzheimers-disease-fact-sheet

"Alzheimer's Disease: Unraveling the Mystery," National Institute on Aging (USA); www.nia.nih.gov/alzheimers/publication/alzheimers-disease-unraveling-mystery

ALZHEIMERS EARLY STAGES New edition: First Steps in Caring and Treatment, by Daniel Kuhn, M.S.W.; www.amazon.co.uk/ALZHEIMERS-EARLY-STAGES-New-Treatment/dp/0897933974/ref=sr_1_6?ie=UTF8&qid=1376924481&sr=8-6&keywords=Daniel+Kuhn

"Care ADvantage®," (Free quarterly for carers of people with Alzheimer's Disease and related illnesses in the USA) Spring 2013 issue, pg. 20: "It's Personal" (see the 2nd scenario: how you know when it is time to relocate a person to a long-term care facility); www.afacareadvantage.org/issues/ca_spring13.pdf

"Caring for a Person with Alzheimer's Disease, Words to Know," National Institute on Aging (USA); www.nia.nih.gov/alzheimers/publication/caring-person-alzheimers-disease/words-know

"Caring for a Person with Alzheimer's Disease, Understanding How AD Changes People – Challenges and Coping Strategies," National Institute on Aging (USA); www.nia.nih.gov/alzheimers/publication/caring-person-ad/understanding-how-ad-changes-people-challenges-and-coping

"Caring for a Person with Alzheimer's Disease," Your Easy- to-Use Guide from the National Institute on Aging (USA); www.nia.nih.gov/sites/default/files/caring_for_a_person_with_alzheimers_disease_0.pdf

"Caring for a person with dementia", Alzheimer's Society UK; http://www.alzheimers.org.uk/site/scripts/documents.php?categoryID=200343

"Dementia Information Resources", Alzheimer's Research UK; http://www.alzheimersresearchuk.org/resources-dementia/

"Home Safety for People with Alzheimer's Disease," National Institute on Aging (USA); www.nia.nih.gov/alzheimers/publication/home-safety-people-alzheimers-disease

"Looking after someone with dementia", NHS Choices Dementia Guide; www.nhs.uk/Conditions/dementia-guide/Pages/dementia-carers.aspx

Stages of Senior Care: Your Step-by-Step Guide to Making the Best Decisions, by Paul & Lori Hogan, founders of Home Instead Senior Care; www.amazon.co.uk/Stages-Senior-Care-Step---Step/dp/0071621091/ref=sr_1_3?ie=UTF8&qid=1376926229&sr=8-3&keywords=stages+of+senior+care

Strength for the Moment: Inspiration for Caregivers, by Lori Hogan; www.amazon.co.uk/Strength-Moment-Inspiration-Lori-Hogan/dp/0307887006/ref=sr_1_1?ie=UTF8&qid=1376926284&sr=8-1&keywords=strength+for+the+moment

"What Happens Next?," A booklet about being diagnosed with Alzheimer's disease or a related disorder, National Institute on Aging (USA); www.nia.nih.gov/sites/default/files/84206ADEARWhatHappensNextEarlyStageBookletab09OCT01_0.pdf

Journal

· · · · · · · · · · · · · · · · · ·

Write down your caregiving experiences.

_____ / _____ / _____
Date

WHAT HAPPENED TODAY?

WAS IT CAUSED BY AN EMOTIONAL, SOCIAL, PHYSICAL OR ENVIRONMENTAL FACTOR?

HOW CAN IT BE PREVENTED TOMORROW?

_____ / _____ / _____
Date

WHAT HAPPENED TODAY?

WAS IT CAUSED BY AN EMOTIONAL, SOCIAL, PHYSICAL OR ENVIRONMENTAL FACTOR?

HOW CAN IT BE PREVENTED TOMORROW?

_____ / _____ / _____
Date

WHAT HAPPENED TODAY?

_____
_____
_____
_____
_____

WAS IT CAUSED BY AN EMOTIONAL, SOCIAL, PHYSICAL OR ENVIRONMENTAL FACTOR?

_____
_____
_____
_____
_____

HOW CAN IT BE PREVENTED TOMORROW?

_____
_____
_____
_____

_____ / _____ / _____

Date

WHAT HAPPENED TODAY?

WAS IT CAUSED BY AN EMOTIONAL, SOCIAL, PHYSICAL OR ENVIRONMENTAL FACTOR?

HOW CAN IT BE PREVENTED TOMORROW?

NOTES

_____ / _____ / _____
Date

WHAT HAPPENED TODAY?

WAS IT CAUSED BY AN EMOTIONAL, SOCIAL, PHYSICAL OR ENVIRONMENTAL FACTOR?

HOW CAN IT BE PREVENTED TOMORROW?

NOTES

_____ / _____ / _____
Date

WHAT HAPPENED TODAY?

WAS IT CAUSED BY AN EMOTIONAL, SOCIAL, PHYSICAL OR ENVIRONMENTAL FACTOR?

HOW CAN IT BE PREVENTED TOMORROW?

NOTES

_____ / _____ / _____
Date

WHAT HAPPENED TODAY?

WAS IT CAUSED BY AN EMOTIONAL, SOCIAL, PHYSICAL OR ENVIRONMENTAL FACTOR?

HOW CAN IT BE PREVENTED TOMORROW?

NOTES

_____ / _____ / _____
Date

WHAT HAPPENED TODAY?

WAS IT CAUSED BY AN EMOTIONAL, SOCIAL, PHYSICAL OR ENVIRONMENTAL FACTOR?

HOW CAN IT BE PREVENTED TOMORROW?

NOTES

_____ / _____ / _____
Date

WHAT HAPPENED TODAY?

_____

_____

_____

_____

_____

WAS IT CAUSED BY AN EMOTIONAL, SOCIAL, PHYSICAL OR ENVIRONMENTAL FACTOR?

_____

_____

_____

_____

_____

HOW CAN IT BE PREVENTED TOMORROW?

_____

_____

_____

_____

_____

NOTES

_____ / _____ / _____
Date

WHAT HAPPENED TODAY?

WAS IT CAUSED BY AN EMOTIONAL, SOCIAL, PHYSICAL OR ENVIRONMENTAL FACTOR?

HOW CAN IT BE PREVENTED TOMORROW?

NOTES

_____ / _____ / _____
Date

WHAT HAPPENED TODAY?

_____
_____
_____
_____
_____

**WAS IT CAUSED BY AN EMOTIONAL, SOCIAL, PHYSICAL
OR ENVIRONMENTAL FACTOR?**

_____
_____
_____
_____
_____

HOW CAN IT BE PREVENTED TOMORROW?

_____
_____
_____
_____
_____

_____ / _____ / _____
Date

WHAT HAPPENED TODAY?

WAS IT CAUSED BY AN EMOTIONAL, SOCIAL, PHYSICAL OR ENVIRONMENTAL FACTOR?

HOW CAN IT BE PREVENTED TOMORROW?

NOTES

_____ / _____ / _____
Date

WHAT HAPPENED TODAY?

WAS IT CAUSED BY AN EMOTIONAL, SOCIAL, PHYSICAL OR ENVIRONMENTAL FACTOR?

HOW CAN IT BE PREVENTED TOMORROW?

NOTES

_____ / _____ / _____

Date

WHAT HAPPENED TODAY?

WAS IT CAUSED BY AN EMOTIONAL, SOCIAL, PHYSICAL OR ENVIRONMENTAL FACTOR?

HOW CAN IT BE PREVENTED TOMORROW?

NOTES

_____ / _____ / _____
Date

WHAT HAPPENED TODAY?

WAS IT CAUSED BY AN EMOTIONAL, SOCIAL, PHYSICAL OR ENVIRONMENTAL FACTOR?

HOW CAN IT BE PREVENTED TOMORROW?

NOTES

_____ / _____ / _____
Date

WHAT HAPPENED TODAY?

_____
_____
_____
_____
_____

WAS IT CAUSED BY AN EMOTIONAL, SOCIAL, PHYSICAL OR ENVIRONMENTAL FACTOR?

_____
_____
_____
_____
_____

HOW CAN IT BE PREVENTED TOMORROW?

_____
_____
_____
_____
_____

_____ / _____ / _____
Date

WHAT HAPPENED TODAY?

WAS IT CAUSED BY AN EMOTIONAL, SOCIAL, PHYSICAL OR ENVIRONMENTAL FACTOR?

HOW CAN IT BE PREVENTED TOMORROW?

NOTES

_____ / _____ / _____
Date

WHAT HAPPENED TODAY?

WAS IT CAUSED BY AN EMOTIONAL, SOCIAL, PHYSICAL OR ENVIRONMENTAL FACTOR?

HOW CAN IT BE PREVENTED TOMORROW?

NOTES

_____ / _____ / _____

Date

WHAT HAPPENED TODAY?

WAS IT CAUSED BY AN EMOTIONAL, SOCIAL, PHYSICAL OR ENVIRONMENTAL FACTOR?

HOW CAN IT BE PREVENTED TOMORROW?

NOTES

_____ / _____ / _____
Date

WHAT HAPPENED TODAY?

WAS IT CAUSED BY AN EMOTIONAL, SOCIAL, PHYSICAL OR ENVIRONMENTAL FACTOR?

HOW CAN IT BE PREVENTED TOMORROW?

_____ / _____ / _____
Date

WHAT HAPPENED TODAY?

WAS IT CAUSED BY AN EMOTIONAL, SOCIAL, PHYSICAL OR ENVIRONMENTAL FACTOR?

HOW CAN IT BE PREVENTED TOMORROW?

NOTES

About Molly Carpenter

....

Author, speaker, trainer and family carer. Molly Carpenter, M.A., brings years of personal and professional senior care experience and training to families dealing with dementia care. Her passionate interest in older adults started early – as a high school student working in an adult day care program – and continues as an adult and a professional. The reality of caring is never far from her experience due to her work in skilled nursing facilities, adult day care centers and continuum of care communities.

In her current role, Carpenter works with a team responsible for ensuring that the Home Instead Senior Care® network's 60,000 caregivers worldwide have the resources necessary to effectively provide quality care in the home and understand the importance of their work enhancing the lives of those they care for. This combined background makes her uniquely qualified to author a book designed specifically to help family carers provide care to those with dementia in the home.

Carpenter's work as part of the team that developed a person-centered approach to Alzheimer's care has been adopted and adapted globally and is critical to the success of the Home Instead care approach for people with Alzheimer's and dementia. This work has been endorsed by leading experts in the Alzheimer's industry and adapted for family carers throughout the world.

Carpenter holds a Bachelor of Science degree in family science with a gerontology specialisation from the University of Nebraska-Lincoln, and a Master's degree in education with a gerontology specialiszation from the University of Nebraska-Omaha. She is currently enrolled in the Human Sciences/Gerontology Ph.D. program at the University of Nebraska-Omaha. Her personal experiences helping to care for her grandmothers have further inspired her career.

Made in the USA
Charleston, SC
27 May 2014